Gilbert Picard
Henri Stierlin (Ed.)

The Roman Empire

Photos: Yvan Butler
Preface: Paolo Portoghesi

Benedikt Taschen

Editor of Series	Henri Stierlin
Plans	Georges Berthoud EPF SIA

© for this edition: Benedikt Taschen Verlag GmbH
© Compagnie du Livre d'Art, S.A.
Editions Office du Livre, Lausanne
Printed in Germany
ISBN 3-8228-9305-6

Contents

Rome and Organic Architecture

Preface by Paolo Portoghesi, architect.

Over the past twenty years the history of modern architecture has been characterized by an attempt to renew the continuity of architectural tradition broken by the violent disputes of the rationalist movement. In 1929, Le Corbusier stated: 'Today I am accused of being a revolutionary. Yet I confess to having had only one master: the past, and only one discipline: the study of the past.' In fact, the study of the past had taught Le Corbusier and other masters of the modern movement to rebel against every

Plan of the Imperial Villa at Piazza Armerina, dating from the Late Empire. About 1:1200.

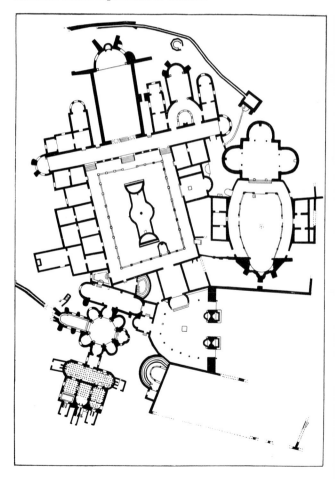

Project for the Municipal Theater at Cagliari, by
Paolo Portoghesi and associates.

formal connection with tradition and to attempt
to start afresh. Over twenty years this healthy
inhibition cleared the ground of all the residue of
eclectic styles, making possible fresh communi-
cation with earlier periods, conditioned by our
own values and technical processes.

Le Corbusier's work bears witness both to the
need for this inhibition and its transitory
character. After the stormy period of World War
II and the first revolutionary phase of modern
art, he began, at Ronchamp, Chandigarh, and
the monastery of La Tourette, to re-examine the

lessons of history in order to restore a basic role
to the past; by a transformed allusion to traditional forms he sought a means of communicating
with the spectator on the basis of his visual
culture and the symbolic values which such
images could acquire. This historical interest is
particularly evident in the case of Frank Lloyd
Wright who frequently sought to recover certain
potentialities which had remained unexpressed
in the stylistic catalogues of the past. The
compositional method of his Johnson Building
appears to be an attempt to extend this method
to a theme characteristic of our own time, with

the fresh results inherent in this meeting.

Roman architecture which had played so important a part in the definition of the fixed rules of nineteenth-century academism, has often been regarded with suspicion by modern architects, especially those dependent on English influences based on the Romantic and neo-Gothic traditions of Ruskin and William Morris. Even Le Corbusier wrote, 'The lesson of Rome is for the wise, those who are aware and can appreciate, who can resist and can control. Rome is the ruin of those who have little aware-

ness.' This observation is still perfectly valid. Roman architecture, according to the way in which it is appreciated, can inspire either conformity, or the acquisition of a method based on a concept of order and arrangement relating isolated buildings to towns and surrounding countryside. The key to Roman architecture lies in the concept of the organic whole: while deriving from the principles of unity and human proportion used by the Greeks in their architecture, it is not wholly contained in these. By virtue of its plastic unity Roman architecture achieves spatial unity. Organic structures are

Project for the Municipal Theater at Cagliari, side elevation of maquette.

Detail of the circular temple at Baalbek.

Detail of the Casa Baldi, Rome, by Paolo Portoghesi.

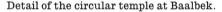

no longer objects set in relation to their natural surroundings and other solid entities; they become pre-eminently hollow forms, containers of highly complex functions organized according to the principles of clarity and hierarchic ordinances. The organism is not only a building but a sequence of buildings or a square, after the manner of the Imperial fora, which is often an independent architectural universe. Such organisms result from loyalty to predetermined laws, thereby revealing the influence of Roman law— laws of aggregate parts based on interdependence.

Amid the numerous facets of Roman architecture modern architects have distinguished two separate tendencies. On the one hand are the central, closed organic structures, static spaces such as the Pantheon and the great temples which have been marvelously translated into reverse terms by modern engineers: starting with massive, hollowed walls, they arrive at Pier Luigi Nervi's elegant, transparent frameworks. Opposed to these are the great narrative compositions—Hadrian's Villa and other buildings whose planned spaces and vistas determine their atmosphere. This part of the Roman heritage which developed under the Late Empire has played a guiding part in the evolution of Western culture, from Roman to Baroque, and is still richly suggestive. Here may be found the prototypes of those great exercises in town-planning which are now dealt with under the name of 'key-points.' It is the prophetic utterance of a language combining law and liberty, conformity and individuality. In the work of Saarinen, Kahn, and Johansen, contemporary architecture has renewed relations with the complex, contradictory culture of the Late Empire and is preparing to recover from it some active, free forces.

Rome 1965

1. Function and Structure of the City

This series aims to define a specific period of architecture by looking at a few of its most characteristic buildings. In this field this may seem somewhat rash, especially when we realize that the latest book on the subject by Luigi Crema deals with over eight hundred examples. On the other hand, the centralization of the Roman Empire resulted in considerable uniformity in its building programmes, so that its cities nearly always consisted of the same types of buildings erected according to almost identical standards. Yet this uniformity vanishes on closer inspection. Only an indifferent architect can fail to sense the skill with which his predecessors managed to interpret their commissions. One of our present aims is to focus on these minute differences, showing that, contrary to a frequently expressed opinion, Roman architecture is not fixed and rigid; research continually produced new solutions and perfected old ones, always with greater boldness and originality.

Architecture, more than any of the other arts, is closely linked with current political and social conditions. Therefore I have chosen to write from the historical rather than the technical point of view (for which I am insufficiently qualified). This attitude seems all the more defensible as the real architects were the political leaders of the Roman people and the professionals were no more than auxiliaries. It has also determined the arrangement of the book: after defining a Roman city as an outward expression of the order of the Empire, I go on to show how the individual buildings correspond to the different categories of this order, and how their aesthetic values and stylistic assertions result from a precise agreement with their aim rather than from an application of abstract principles.

Thus a Roman building reveals the spirit of the Empire as accurately as the writings of a Roman historian, and each one may be considered a reflection of the Empire as a whole.

Roman architecture is essentially one of cities, though there were, in fact, some large country estates of great interest. One of these, Hadrian's Villa at Tibur (Tivoli), is of special note as it was an imperial residence. The majority of the buildings and monuments discussed here were

Rome: plan of Forum of Augustus (after Kähler). About 1:2000.

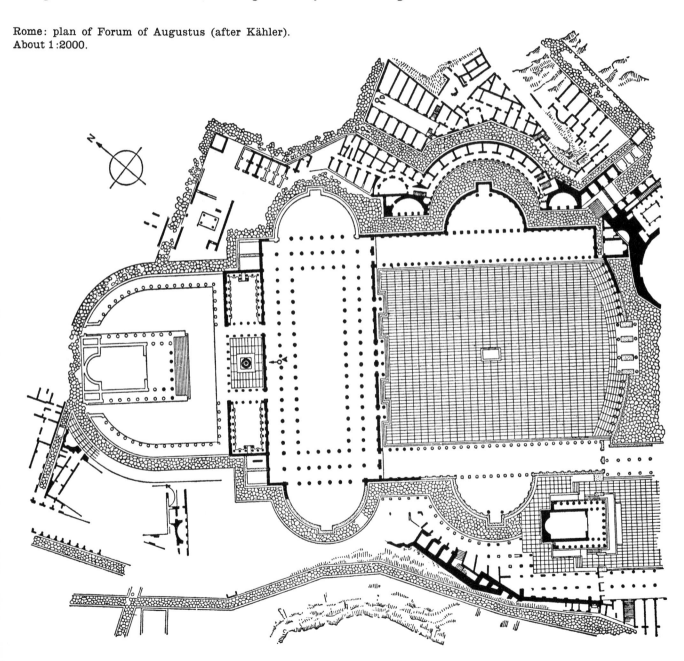

designed for fairly large urban communities and, for this reason, we must start with an analysis of a Roman city and its wholly unique features.

The Development of Rome

For over three centuries, Rome was no different from any other small town on the Italian peninsula. Its origin dates from the mid-eighth century B.C. when it was a confederation of villages built on hills above a marshy plain skirted by the Tiber. In the seventh century the draining of the valleys enabled the federation to make one of them into a political center—the Forum, which was to remain the heart of an ever increasing state until the end of antiquity. Shortly afterwards, the Etruscans became masters of the city and gave it its first monuments; traces of these have allowed a fairly accurate reconstruction of the Capitol, the most important of them, dedicated in 509 B.C. Severe political struggles, both internal and external, followed the expulsion of the foreign dynasty in the same year, and slowed down the growth of the city for three centuries. Though victorious over its neighbors and mistress of a now extensive state, Rome remained a political and military capital with little economic activity until the year 200. The only important monuments were the temples enriched with captured plunder; some were built after Etruscan, others after Greek, models. The Forum, the only political and cultural center, became congested. Not until the first century B.C. did a series of authoritarian governments begin to instil some sense into this chaos swarming with nearly one million inhabitants. Yet none ever managed to bring total order to the largest center of population known to the ancient world.

Rome also gradually became a focal point of culture and, from the beginning of the Empire, created a way of life copied by the entire world. Its military role diminished, however, as the frontiers of its power extended. Economically the

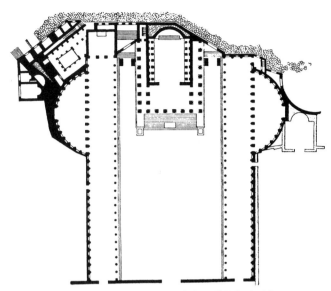

Rome: plan of Trajan's Forum (after Kähler). About 1:2000.

city became little more than a consumer on a gigantic scale. Its religious function was more or less identified with politics and culture until Christianity triumphed.

The Colonies

Rome reproduced itself abroad with extraordinary vigor. Towards the middle of the fourth century B.C. it overflowed the borders of Italy and assumed a different character. It was no longer a question of keeping guard over the weak chinks of the Empire (apart from a few exceptional cases) but of disposing of a surplus population that could no longer be supported by its native soil. During the civil wars and under the early Empire, the aim of colonization was to provide for the conquerors at the expense of the conquered. From the beginning of the second century A.D. colonization underwent a complete change of nature and aim. Now it became an instrument of political and social progress for the descendants of the conquered. Never have colonies been so numerous; there were some hundreds of them in provinces like Asia Minor

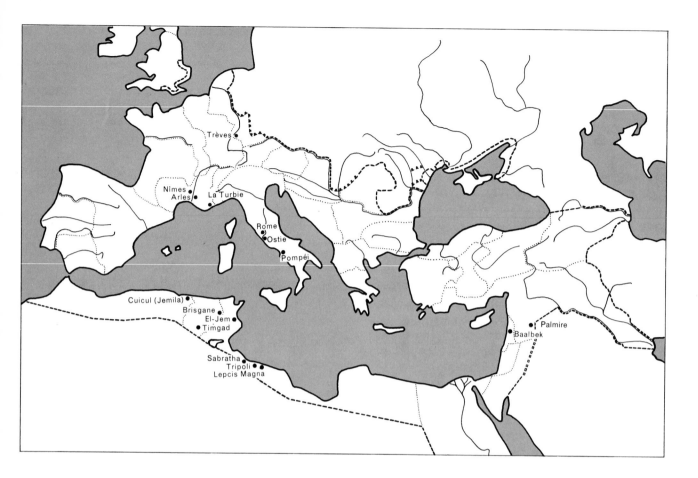

Map of the Roman world showing the chief towns
cited in the book.

and North Africa. The urban centers were not
new creations but ancient cities in Roman dress;
similarly, their inhabitants were descended
from the natives, but had requested and received
co-citizenship with the Romans.

These offshoots of Rome enjoyed functions
similar to the parent city, but structurally were
completely different. They were pre-eminently
political and cultural centers where the bourgeoisie held the power of government and administered large areas of territory with great

fairness, spreading abroad a fashion for the
Roman way of life. None of these cities were
great centers of industrial production, for
important industries were to be found in the
country rather than the town.

Some cities, particularly ports, carried on
commercial activities which resulted in large
warehouses like the Horrea Epagathiana at
Ostia. Generally, however, Roman cities existed
more or less directly off the land and the vast
scale of their building operations was financed

by the surplus from agricultural revenues, and rendered possible by the almost complete absence of wars for two centuries. The maintenance expenses of an army which was only posted on frontiers, and the drain on labor which these forces represented, were relatively unimportant, considering that they consisted of no more than 400,000 men throughout the Empire.

Fortified towns disappeared, except on the frontiers, until after the invasions of the third century which, in parts such as Gaul, resulted in a basic change of population, nearly always after a prolonged period of destruction; but such events did not affect the most civilized provinces till much later. Nor did religion dominate urban life except sometimes in the East, as at Baalbek. At Nîmes, a Gallic nature sanctuary which had formed the center of the early native settlement was transformed into a place of amusement. Often temples were conspicuously placed in the center of a city, but these were more usually devoted to political and cultural activities rather than to religious purposes. The places of worship of the mystical religions, among which must be included Christian churches until the end of the third century, were usually of little note and, apart from the temples of Mithras, offered no real architectural characteristics. Very often they were no more than ordinary, almost unaltered houses. In Africa, where the traditional forms of Punic worship were still observed, the temples were, surprisingly, in the suburbs, and the Celtic gods were worshipped in the open country.

Thus the Roman 'urbs' was very different from the cities of Egypt and the East overshadowed by their temples. The 'urbs' had a far more natural connection with the Greek 'polis:' as with the Greeks the town center was a square meant for the assembly of the townspeople and the discussion of public affairs. With the establishment of the Empire, however, the forum attracted the citizens less than did the theaters,

amphitheaters, baths and basilicas. Thus one of the basic tasks of Roman architects was the creation and development of these places of assembly and recreation for which they worked out completely new structural and aesthetic solutions. Indeed Rome may truly be called a city of parasites. The common people were largely encouraged to be idle by the government; they lived off income from capital collected by their ancestors when they conquered the world. Provincial cities lived off the country but, when they were very highly populated, as was the case in the richest provinces, there was no question of brutal opposition between an exploited rural proletariat and an idle urban bourgeoisie.

Geometrical Town-planning

The functions of cities were very similar, whether it was Rome or a modest provincial settlement. But the well organized town-plans of the colonial cities were in complete contrast to the confusion of the capital.

Timgad (Thamugadi), dating from the early second century, is usually taken as an example of a typical Roman town. An aerial view shows the strict geometrical layout of this colony, built on the upland plains of southern Algeria near the Aures mountains. The built-up area consists of a perfect square divided by two axial streets running at right angles to form a capital T. The 'Cardo' runs from north to south, the 'Decumanus' from east to west. At the point of their intersection is the forum, a vast rectangular square with the theater on one side. Secondary streets, parallel to the two axes, outline square sections of equal size, accommodating private houses and public buildings.

This type of surveyor's plan derived from an ancient Italian tradition and may already be found in some Etruscan cities of the sixth century, such as Marzabotto. It probably originated in Asia Minor where the Ionians adopted it long before Hippodamus of Miletus, who has recently been credited with its invention. Its success with the Romans may have been due to both religious and military reasons.

The regular town-plan of the Romans may be seen to have evolved, although along different lines, from the rationalist genius of the Greeks. Nor need we believe that it was as strictly applied as some text books would have it. We have already seen that Rome was never subjected to it. On the other hand, its basic principles may be found at Pompeii, Alba Fucens, and at Ostia which was founded shortly after the middle of the fourth century. Almost

A Roman camp, showing the right-angled layout found throughout the towns of the Empire.

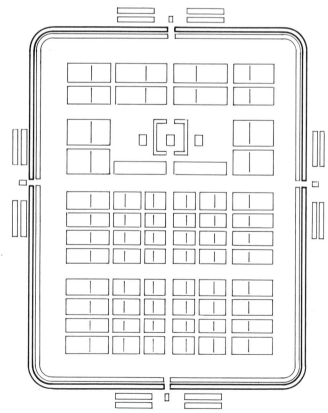

invariably, however, there were compromises with the nature of the ground, which prevented its complete realization. Also, once the city was inhabited, the claims of everyday life asserted themselves and tended to upset the fine layout. Timgad, for example, did not remain the carefully surveyed colony commanded by the Emperor Trajan. Before the end of the second century A.D. large suburbs sprang up all round the city, making it more than four times as large. Moreover, these suburbs were grouped around roads which linked the city with neighboring towns; they did not run at right angles nor were they orientated like those in the center. In these outer districts were important buildings, indispensable to the life of the city; they included the Capitol, the two largest 'thermae' and, right in the south, a magnificent sanctuary built in the reign of Septimius Severus around a health-giving spring which had helped to attract the colonists. This sanctuary is now enclosed by a Byzantine fortress.

As a general rule, however, straight streets intersecting at right angles were an ideal which every municipality strove to attain. The towns which had acquired the honorary title of colony made special efforts to resemble the real colonies which had been erected on virgin soil according to a regular plan. If necessary, entire old quarters were unhesitatingly destroyed in order to rebuild to a regular plan. Even in the case of historic towns, architects were not checked out of any respect for the past: during the Empire, the Greek city at Marseilles was completely pulled down. Where the ground was uneven there was no hesitation in using the most expensive methods of terracing to replace the slope by superimposed flat stretches linked by staircases. The town of Praeneste (Palestrina), just over twenty miles south-east of Rome, is one of the oldest examples of this type of undertaking. The complex stands on the steep slope of a spur of the Apennines dominating the town,

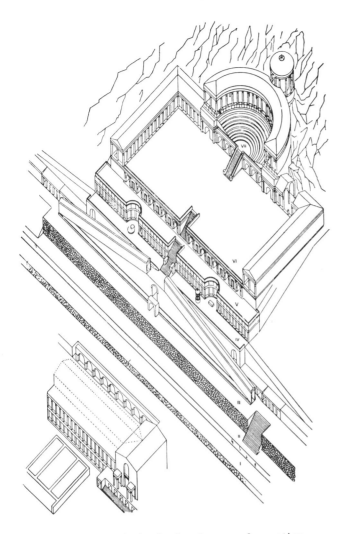

Praeneste (Palestrina): the first large-scale creation of Roman town-planning.

and near the cave where the goddess was supposed to deliver her oracles. Great ramps lead first to a narrow terrace whose upper side is bordered by an inward curving colonnade forming two hemicycles. From here a staircase rises to a second terrace giving on to a huge square, the Cortina: this, too, has a colonnade surrounding it on three sides, and is dominated by a theater hewn from the living rock. This mag-

nificent pyramidal construction may be considered the first grandiose conception of Roman town-planning. The contemporary Temple of Hercules at Tibur (Tivoli), on the other hand, has more in common with architectural landscape. In 44 or 42 B.C., when the triumvirs (in accordance with the wishes of Julius Caesar) decided to build a colony on the site of Carthage, the hills dominating the coastal plain were systematically levelled out and one of them, destined for the Capitol, had the periphery of its summit rearranged to form a perfect rectangle. Works of this nature resulted in giving the uneven terrain a layout as regular as at Timgad.

Development of Towns

Cuicul (Djemila), in the former Kingdom of Numidia, was a small colony whose natural development was restricted by its site. It was one of the last with a military function, designed to keep watch over a mountainous region of great strategical importance, with a turbulent population. The officers charged with its foundation, about the end of the first century B.C., chose a site that was easy to defend: a narrow plateau between two ravines. This type of spur was a frequent choice for antique settlements, but was usually avoided by the Roman townplanners. The first nucleus of Cuicul was triangular in shape, one side formed by the long straight street called the 'Cardo' on account of its orientation and because it skirted one of the sides of the forum which was clearly not the axis of the plan. This developed completely only to the east of the street, and consisted of rectangular island blocks which surrounded the public square on three sides. A retaining wall forming an acute angle with the 'Cardo' sealed off the southern side of the spur. A century after the foundation, turbulence in the surrounding countryside more or less calmed down and the inhabitants, now nearly doubled in number, created a suburb by extending the main street; this was larger than the town center. Here, in the last years of the second century, an important set of baths was built, and a theater was constructed right outside the city in a hollow of the steep slope on the eastern ravine. Later, in the Severan period, the planners decided to make a new town center, and a new forum was created whose trapezoidal shape was determined by the old wall transformed into a raised arcade.

Leptis Magna

The economic and demographic development of African cities in the second and third centuries confronted town-planners with complex problems. Timgad and Cuicul were too modest to allow ambitious plans, but Leptis Magna, on the

Leptis Magna: the market, plan and reconstruction (after Bandinelli and Caffarelli). About 1:1250.

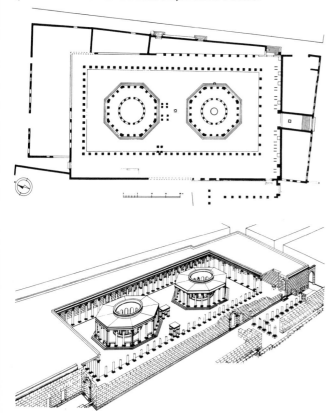

eastern border of Tripolitania, was a very different case. In the seventh century B.C. the Phoenicians had established themselves on the peninsula forming the upper lip of the estuary of the Cinyps, now the river Lebda. Situated at the end of a route across the Sahara through the Fezzan, the city soon prospered. When the Punic settlement was taken over by Caesar in 46 B.C., its center was probably a roughly rectangular square, the old forum, and it is likely that the town already extended to the site of the future theater which lies over a necropolis. The public square was at the end of a road which followed the river bed for some distance and had to effect a quick change into a street along its final stretch. The Augustan city with its market, shops and its theater, developed to the north of this road and west of the square. During the first century A.D., the forum was repaved and surrounded by temples. The town then expanded along the main axis which was doubled on the north-east by a parallel avenue and intersected by streets at right angles, thus creating an outline plan. Arches dedicated to Tiberius and Trajan made it a triumphal avenue corresponding to a 'Cardo.' In Nero's reign the port was improved by major harbor installations and, under Hadrian, the town, which had meanwhile become a Roman colony, was provided with baths that included the most modern refinements after the pattern of those at Rome.

Such was the state of the city in A.D. 193 when Septimius Severus, a native of Leptis, became Emperor. A new plan drawn up was destined both to increase the business capacities of the city and to give it an appearance suitable to the birthplace of an Emperor. It was decided to deflect the course of the river and change its mouth into an artificial harbor basin similar to the one at Ostia. The dry bed was turned into a wide avenue with arcades like those of eastern cities, and later a new civic center with a forum and basilica was built adjoining it. Hadrian's

Leptis Magna: interior of the Severan Basilica (after Bandinelli and Caffarelli).

baths were integrated with the new quarter, which was approached by an imposing street at right angles to the triumphal avenue. The intersection was marked by an arch of four bays whose sculptured decoration is one of the most remarkable manifestations of Roman Imperial art: a triumph in sculpture of primitive or baroque aesthetic conception which henceforth paved the way for the flowering of Byzantine art. The avenue with the arcades became the axis of the new city, since a quarter equal in area to, or maybe larger than, the old town and still unexcavated, came into being south of the port on the old right bank of the river, stretching as far as the circus and amphitheater, well over a mile from the new forum.

The whole scheme was on a lavish scale and elegantly decorated. Of particular interest to a town-planner is the solution adopted for the integration into the existing plan of the baths and the new avenue, whose course was determined by that of the old river bed. A 'nymphaeum' or monumental fountain was placed on the spot marking the change of direction, serving as a pivot for the two different orientations.

This grandiose, slightly pretentious metropolis was severely harassed by nomad raids from the fourth century onwards, and then by a Byzantine occupation that left as its traces a city wall and several churches. Finally, in the early Middle Ages, the city was abandoned and covered by sand carried along by the river now returned to its natural bed. As a result the Severan forum and basilica were preserved and may now be seen almost intact. The harbor, too, can now be seen in all its detail.

Siting of Buildings

In our survey of Leptis we have been introduced to almost all the buildings necessary to life in a Roman city. The forum, which could be twice the size of the one at Leptis, was always surrounded by the buildings needed for the administration of daily life: the 'curia,' the seat of the municipal senate, and the basilica where law cases were heard; the temples of the gods who watched over the city and of the Imperial cult; the market, which served as a center for part of the business community, whereas the remainder, including craftsmen, were scattered in shops usually flanking the hallways of private houses; and, finally, the buildings designed for pleasure—baths, theaters and amphitheaters for gladiatorial fights and wild beast hunts. There were no strict rules regarding their siting, but the forum was usually in the center if the nature of the ground was favorable. Amphitheaters and circuses were almost always on the fringes of towns, along with the sanctuaries of gods who were not wholly Roman—or else thought to be dangerous—such as Mars or Vulcan. Much attention was paid to the positioning of buildings, both from an aesthetic point of view, and so that they might benefit from a maximum of sun in winter, there being no form of domestic heating except in the northern provinces.

Streets

We still have to recreate the atmosphere of a Roman street, not an easy thing to do when surveying extensive excavations. We must visit the New Excavations on the Strada dell' Abbondanza at Pompeii to find façades with their elevations and painted decoration completely restored. A Roman street, at any rate in Italy, was as alive and colorful then as streets in present-day Naples. The houses usually had no opening on the ground floor apart from the door, but their upper storeys were provided with windows, balconies, verandas and loggias. Their fronts were daubed with crude, vividly colored frescoes, very different from the skilfully executed interior decorations. They represented the gods worshipped by ordinary citizens—the Pompeian Venus in her chariot drawn by elephants, Mercury, Hercules accompanied by a little pig, the genius of the Emperor. The merchants and craftsmen were portrayed at work in their booths, and electoral agents had their candidates' manifestos boldly painted over all the rest. Later on, at Ostia, this form of color was replaced by contrasting effects between the bricks of the walls and the architectural elements of dark or white stone. Roman cities were never dominated by the white marble facings of modern neo-classic buildings—seldom found in Greece either—nor by the pure white plaster coatings of Moslem houses.

Colonnades and Fountains

There will be little further mention of streets and squares in this book, but we must bear in mind that the Romans spent much of their time strolling along the Via Sacra. Activities in the street could not be carried out unprotected from the full sun any more than from the violent downpours that so frequently occur in Mediterranean countries. Colonnades were therefore essential features of Roman cities. They lined every square and often streets as well in the manner of eastern cities: the most notable examples which survive are at Palmyra and Apameia.

Another decorative feature of town-planning which may be considered typically Roman is the fountain. Of course, Greek cities had their springs, but it was in the late Hellenistic age that such remarkable strides were made in the technique of hydraulics. This progress permitted skilful effects which Roman constructions of rubble and cement could show off to spectacular advantage. The result was a series of monumental fountains known, more or less accurately, as 'nymphaea,' the immediate forerunners of the countless fountains of modern Rome.

Sometimes on Italian and, more often, on African sites the 'green belts' — another typical Roman feature — have been superseded by modern growths which revive the glories of the dead ruins. When Caesar bequeathed to the people the gardens which he had originally created for his own use (as had done Lucullus and Pompey) he was the first to provide them with such an amenity. Private gardens, like those at Pompeii, were seldom found, apart from the sacred groves of temples or suburban cemeteries where the mausoleums were often surrounded by sacred gardens. At Ostia, however, the builders of huge apartment blocks had the very modern idea of surrounding their buildings with 'green belts' to compensate the tenants for the disadvantage of being crowded together.

Plates

The Pont du Gard, near Nîmes

21 The combined bridge and aqueduct with its three
to rows of superimposed arches.
23 Functional architecture of the Augustan period.

Timgad (Algeria)

24 Aerial view of the layout of the town. In the center, Trajan's original colony, in the form of a square subdivided into smaller square blocks by straight streets crossing at right angles.

25 The Arch of Trajan, from the town side. The monumental gateway in baroque style makes use of the lively contrasts of light and shade caused by the African sun.

Arles: The Cryptoportici

26 Subterranean galleries probably used to provide access to shops, below the level of the edge of the Forum. Each gallery is divided into two aisles. The roof consists of a barrel vault of rubble construction.

27 The galleries are lit by window openings in the curve of the vault.

Oil Factory at Brisgane, near Tebessa (Algeria)

28 The effect presented by this weird construction is due to the disappearance of the courses of small stones which used to fill the empty spaces.

29 In the foreground, lintels supporting a wall of large blocks above the door. In the background, the arches of the interior courtyard.

30 Series of arches bordering the courtyard.

31 Each pillar receives the thrust of two arches, transmitted by their key-stones. They also support the straight lintel which passes above the arches and is level with their key-stones without resting directly on them.

Ostia: The Horrea Epagathiana

32 Courtyard of Epagathus, a rich Eastern Greek merchant of the port of Ostia. On the wall, on either side of an opening with a depressed arch, two niches in the form of aedicules.

33 Detail of one of the niches, which probably housed small statues of gods.

34 Façade to the street. A great vaulted doorway framed in a classic type decorative structure of brick.

35 Detail of door capital. An interpretation in stuccoed brick of a composite capital. A Roman creation of the late first century A.D.

36 In the Hellenistic period, a courtyard bordered by galleries formed an essential part of a commercial building. The groined vaults are supported on four-sided pillars.

Rome: Trajan's Markets

37 Façade of the great hemicycle overlooking the Forum, a very fine example of a concave arched front. On the ground floor are booths. Above, the windows of the promenade giving access to shops.

38 General view from the Via Biberatica overlooking the hemicycle and leading to the basilica.

39 Entrance to one of the staircases. The travertine doorposts and lintel stand out against the brick wall.

40 The three-storeyed construction of shops overlooking the Via Biberatica, showing the brick lintels inserted between the pillars. This technique allowed buildings of several storeys to be put up without the help of timber scaffolding.

41 Shop-fronts facing the gallery of the great hemicycle.

42 Detail of the brick pillars.

43 The Basilica of Trajan, a vast market hall, roofed by a series of adjoining groined vaults which buttress one another. It houses two storeys of shops.

44 The groined vaults of the upper floor of shops.

Pont du Gard Elevation 1:1000.

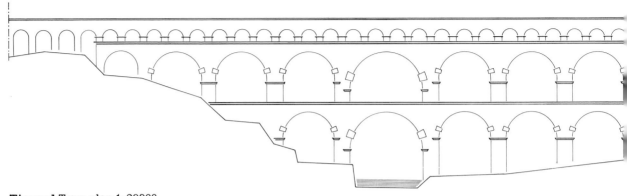

Timgad Town plan 1:20000.
A. Arch of Trajan.

0 5o 1oo 2oo   4oo   6oo
                                        M
                                        FT
0 2oo 4oo   1ooo   2ooo

Arch of Trajan at Timgad
Plan and elevation 1:300.

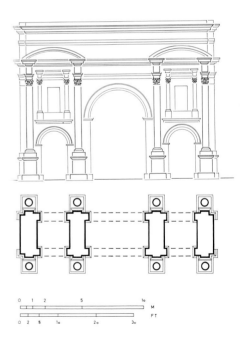

0 1 2   5   1o
                              M
                              FT
0 2 5   1o   2o   3o

The Cryptoportici at Arles Plan 1:1000.
Longitudinal and transverse sections 1:200.

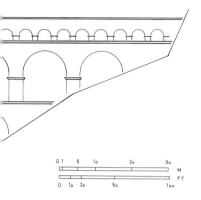

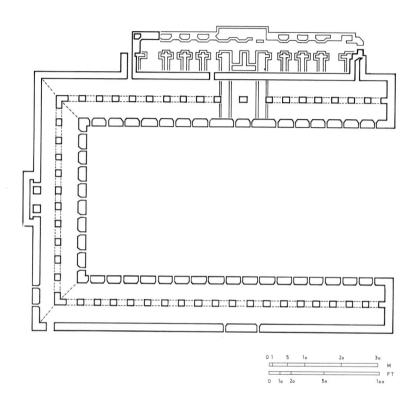

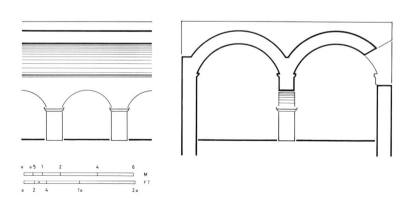

Notes

Timgad

This Roman colony was founded by Trajan in 100 A.D. in the lofty plateaux north of the Aures Mountains for a group of veterans of the 3rd Augustan legion which supplied the garrison for Lambaesis. The choice of site was due to its proximity to a spring whose waters were supposed to be health-giving. The central district, corresponding to the original colony, is strictly orientated in accordance with the rules of the Roman surveyors, and its east-west axis consists of a wide street bordered by colonades, the decumanus maximus. Half-way along it, the cardo maximus leads towards the north. South of the decumanus, the central section of the town is taken up with the rectangular forum, bordered on its east side by the law courts: this is a secular square, the only religious building being a fairly small temple. Immediately to the south, the side of an isolated hill was dug out to provide the cavea of the theater which extended to the boundaries of the colony. The most outstanding of the other public buildings sited on the planned perimeter is the library, which bears witness to the intellectual activity of this outpost town of the Empire.

Timgad was originally planned for small landowners of moderate resources, but the great economic expansion of Africa in the second half of the second and most of the third century resulted in increased wealth and an appreciable rise in population—it swelled to about fifteen thousand. Leading citizens wanted to beautify their houses, built round colonnaded courtyards in accordance with the usual African plan, whose chief difference from the Italian was the absence of an atrium.

The chief form of decoration used in the third century was an original style of mosaic making abundant use of the acanthus motif. The citizens' particular aim, however, was to endow the community with buildings designed to house public amenities: these included the great thermae which were constructed in the suburbs that grew up, following no set plan, along the roads leading into the town. Markets and places of worship such as the Capitol were also built here. The efforts of the inhabitants were especially directed towards the tutelary divinities of the spring, which was transformed in the early third century during the reign of the African Emperor, Septimius Severus, into a lavish building, both spa and temple. When, in the fourth century, there was a general conversion to Christianity, churches also arose in the suburbs: this duality recalls that the peace of the city was later disturbed by bitter struggles between Catholics and schismatic Donatists.

The conquering Vandals brought ruin to Timgad about 530, and the city was practically destroyed by the mountain tribesmen of the Aures. The Romanized farmers for whom the town was a center did not, however, resign themselves to the loss of their civilization. They willingly received the soldiers of Justinian under the leadership of the patrician, Solomon, who transformed the former sanctuary of the spring into a powerful fortress. Thus protected, the Roman way of life continued until its final submergence in the seventh century, due to a coalition between Aures tribesmen and Sahara nomads.

Apollodorus of Damascus, The Architect of Trajan

Apollodorus of Damascus is the last of the great Imperial architects known to us by name, and we also have good evidence regarding his life and career. Unlike his predecessors, of Latin origin, Apollodorus, was an Eastern Greek. This suggests that he introduced to Rome the techniques of Hellenistic architecture which had been preserved in his native country. For two centuries, however, the chief developments in the art of building had occurred in Italy, and the materials which Apollodorus had at his disposal, including fired bricks and rubble bound by cement, were quite unlike those used by the architects of the Seleucids and the kings of Pergamon. The structures he had to deal with, vaults in particular, had been discovered and perfected in Rome. It is true that there had been remarkable architectural development in Syria and Asia Minor in the late first and early second centuries, but the resulting buildings show much evidence of borrowings from Western architecture along with original techniques. Besides, there is no proof of any sort that Apollodorus was trained in his native land. His first appearance is with Trajan in the war against the Dacians when he built, in 104-5, a huge bridge across the Danube, which is depicted on Trajan's Column. Like many other Roman architects, Apollodorus received his primary training as a military engineer: this was particularly useful at a time when the army was practically the only organization which had up-to-date mechanical building aids at its disposal. After the war he was commissioned to construct Trajan's Forum and Markets (106 to 113).

Oil factory at Brisgane Longitudinal and transverse sections, and plan 1 :250.

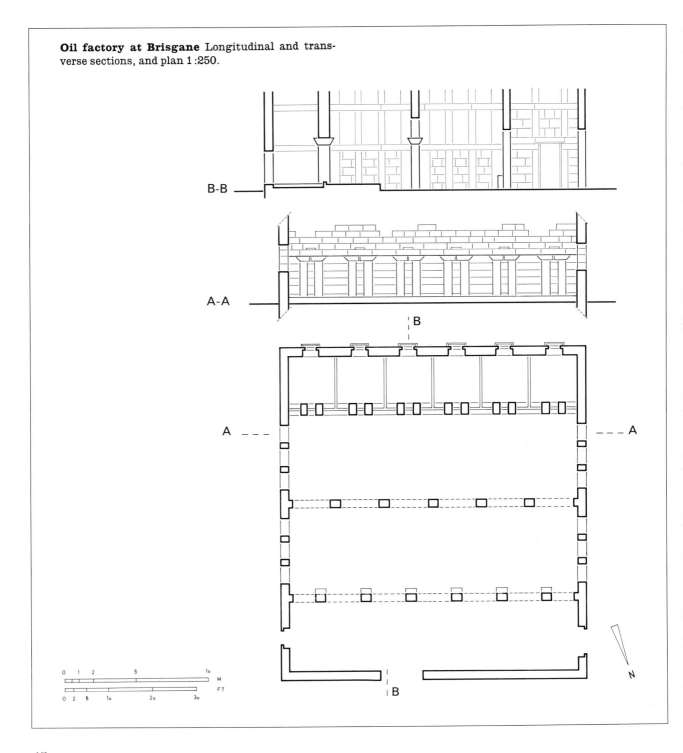

Trajan's Markets, Rome Plan 1:1500 and section 1:500.

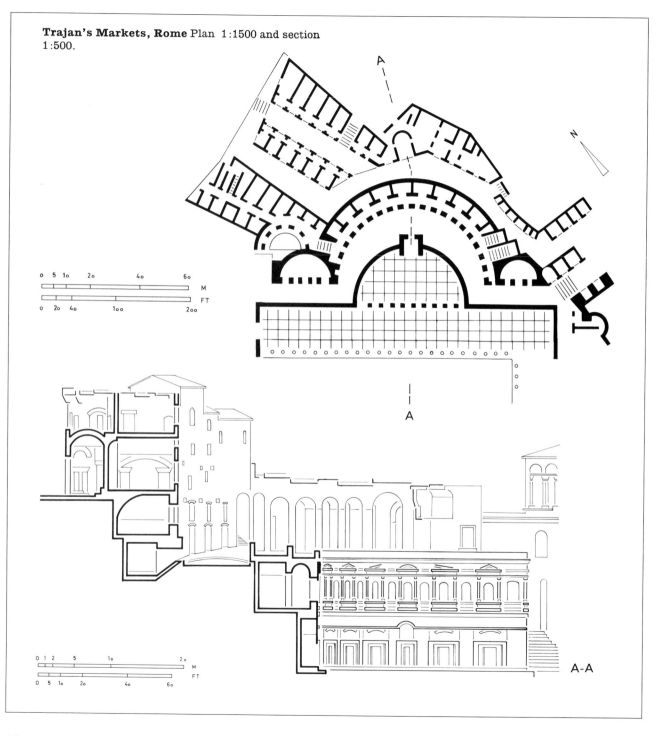

M
FT

A-A

2. A Functional Architecture

'Just compare the vital, massive piles of our countless aqueducts with the Pyramids which serve no purpose, or with the useless, yet universally renowned works of the Greeks.' This sentence from Frontinus' 'De aquis urbis Romae' sounds crude, yet it reveals the most original characteristic of Roman architecture— one that distinguishes it from that of all other periods except nineteenth century Europe during the Industrial Revolution. Rome alone, while mindful of her gods and princes, was desirous of ensuring, for the millions whom she governed, material prosperity and collective comforts. This aim, so modern-sounding, will be dealt with in a later chapter. First of all, let us turn to buildings linked with economic life.

All of these have in common a powerful austerity which, as we shall see later, also tends to assert itself in other types of building. This principle is inherent in the basic laws of the art of architecture as conceived by the Romans. Their architects worked according to the same fundamentals as their soldiers and administrators. The real Roman architect was both a politician and a soldier who had the help of technicians: their monuments do not bear the name of an architect, but of an Emperor or magistrate, and this is only fair because it was the holder of public office who was the real author ('auctor') of the building. This does not mean to say that the real architects were not held in high esteem. On the other hand, Vitruvius, Severus, and Celer who carried out Nero's projects, Rabirius who worked for Domitian, and Apollodorus of Damascus, the designer of Trajan's Forum, were never more than aides and counselors.

It must not be supposed that the statesmen and administrators followed the work of their aides from a remote distance. Evidence on this point is provided by Frontinus. He was first praetor, then successively consul, general in Germany, and civil and military governor of the whole of Britain. In 97 A.D., when over sixty, this experienced senator became superintendent of the aqueducts of Rome, one of the highest posts in the state. A treatise he wrote is a model of technical accuracy and shows that its author possessed an astonishing knowledge of mathematics and physics at a time when education was essentially literary.

These great administrators had the public interest as their basic aim, but their merit lies in not having sacrificed the beautiful to the practical, but in having created a new aesthetic, expressive of the power of their work.

Opus Caementicium and Dynamic Architecture

Roman architects used applied decoration, especially in the interiors of their buildings, which resulted in magnificent baroque effects, the meaning and development of which will be discussed in a later chapter. The exterior façades, however, usually owe their beauty to power of material and interplay of points of stress freely exposed. The Greeks based their architecture on the use of large stone blocks with their joins exposed: this was expressive of nobility and integrity but its range was limited. The Romans did not hew and combine separate blocks as in a jigsaw puzzle, but made a homogenous mass by dipping small stones in cement. This type of rubble allowed them a full range of dynamics and formed the core of their buildings. It was covered with a facing within which were, at first, large blocks bound by mortar: these were soon replaced by small stones and, later on, by bricks. This basic revolution in the art of building was as important as the adoption of iron in the nineteenth century, and took place during the third and second centuries B.C. It was caused primarily by a desire to build solidly and cheaply and was probably inherited from the Carthaginians. Very soon it became clear that the use of concrete favored the construction of vaults which originated in the Near East and the pre-Hellenic Aegean. Neglected by the Greeks, it was perfected and brought into general use by the Etruscans, especially the arch made from large blocks, a form of construction maintained by the Romans; the Temple of Diana at Nîmes is a fine example of a barrel vault employing large stones, dating from the end of the first century A.D. The typical Roman vault, however, was made of concrete, monolithic and almost indestructible. Their engineers continued to perfect its construction, either by means of combinations allowing an indefinitely increased span, or by bold interior reductions of weight permitting a skilful interplay of light. This type of roofing obviously transformed the basic lines of their buildings. Curves were substituted for right angles, both in plan and elevation, giving rise to a multilinear architecture that formed the basis of the baroque aesthetic. The solidity of concrete and the balance of its inner forces allowed the size of buildings to increase indefinitely and permitted the builders to master any unevenness of the ground by resisting its thrust. Because of these techniques, the Roman architects were able to remodel the landscape—unlike the Greeks, who were subservient to it. They could also give their buildings colossal proportions which have led them to be compared with those of ancient Egypt, though these were achieved with the help of far cruder techniques.

The Pont du Gard

This famous aqueduct, completed about 20 B.C. and commissioned by Agrippa, was designed to carry the waters of a spring near Uzès to Nîmes. The part played by water in the collective amenities typical of Roman civilization will be discussed later. It is, however, a mistake to picture the aqueducts as consisting of lofty arches after the superb example of the Pont du Gard. In actual fact they were conduits, pipes made of rubble, which linked the springs with the places they were to serve. The main problem was to establish the slope most suited to the flow of water throughout a course that often lay across very hilly regions, as the best springs rose in the mountains. Moreover, the Roman engineers seldom used pumps, though these had been invented by the hydraulic experts of Alexandria.

One of the few occasions when they had recourse to such a device was in the water supply for Lyons. The conduit was usually accommodated in a cutting where the ground rose higher and was raised up over depressions. As a general rule, arches were only used where it crossed valleys, as in the case of the Pont du Gard. It was soon apparent, however, that the arches protected the water from theft and contamination and, especially in the neighborhood of Rome, steps were taken to keep most of the conduit above the ground.

The conduit which formed the heart of the aqueduct may be considered one of the most truly Roman creations. The peasants of Latium and southern Etruria were forced, from an early date, to dig drainage channels in the volcanic soil to decontaminate the swamps which kept on forming so easily in this region. In the case of Rome, the first settlement perched on the hills could not expand into the valleys until the streams that originally flowed through them had been canalized. This was done in the sixth century but only very crudely at first, the Cloaca Maxima remaining open for several centuries. Its first covering was of planks: the vault which survives today only dates from the late Republic.

The idea of using conduits to bring water in as well as to evacuate it, materialized in the late sixth century B.C. The censor, Appius Claudius Caecus, one of the greatest politicians of his time and a founder of imperialism, was responsible both for the road linking Rome with Campania and the 'aqua Appia' which brought in water from a spring some ten miles away from the capital. This channel was dug out of the tufa, wherever possible, and in loose soil consisted of blocks of stone pierced by a center tube and joined one to another.

There was no basic difference between the bridge of an aqueduct and an ordinary bridge, another typical product of Roman architecture. It was not until 179 B.C. that the censors built a bridge over the Tiber with stone piers and a wooden platform; and in 142 B.C. the piers were linked by arches. So it was about the middle of the second century B.C., when Roman architects were beginning to realize all that could be done with the use of vaults, that the idea occurred of using them to solve a technical problem of supreme importance. The arched bridge was the only type capable of standing up to the sudden floods experienced in Mediterranean countries.

An ordinary bridge has a single row of arches, but the Pont du Gard has three, one above the other. In this it differs from most other aqueducts, which only have two. Thus its proportions are very different from those of the famous aqueduct at Segovia, whose lower arches are very high and narrow; those of the Pont du Gard, only six in all, have wide openings, 52 feet to 70 feet compared with a height of 66 feet. This feature is clearly due to the fact that the aqueduct crosses a swift flowing river unlike that at Segovia which is built over dry land.

The first stage is really a bridge which still carries a road and has breakwaters on the sides of the piers facing upstream. The second storey is almost exactly double the first: it is the same height and consists of eleven arches instead of six because of its wider span. The middle arches, however, are directly above those of the bridge and have exactly the same dimensions. With the third storey comes a break in a rhythm which would otherwise become too monotonous; it is only 28 feet high and consists of thirty-five arches each of which is about half the total elevation. They play a purely aesthetic part, since the conduit could either have been placed directly on the second level or on a solid wall. This is the only decorative element conceded by the architect. Nowhere else is there any form of ornament, not even the niches which are so often hollowed out in the angles between the arches of Roman bridges. Evidently the architect felt that even the most restrained form of decoration would detract from the powerful effect of the whole composition, emphasized by the quality of the building material. For the aqueduct also differs from most others in that it is built of large blocks without mortar. The arched vaults have elongated keystones which adjoin one another but are not cemented together. In order to stress the sobriety of the construction, the architect has left the corbels used to support the scaffolding projecting from the piers. There are also some keystones, jutting out from the spring of each arch above the plain cornice separating it from the pillar. The architect wished to show his special skill in harmonizing his composition with the attractive landscape surrounding it. Those art historians who have said that the Romans, unlike the Greeks, never took advantage of natural beauty, have probably never seen the Pont du Gard.

The Cryptoportici of Arles

In the Rhône valley at Arles another masterpiece of Roman functional architecture contemporary with the Pont du Gard has come to light. This consists of three underground galleries in the shape of a U: the vertical branches are almost 295 feet high and the horizontal branch 200 feet long. Each gallery is 28 feet wide and 14½ feet high and is roofed by paired barrel vaults which are supported on one side by one of the walls and on the other by a series of square pillars set along the axis of the gallery. These pillars are linked by semi-circular arches whose construction and proportions are reminiscent of the lower courses of the Pont du Gard.

The building has not yet been thoroughly surveyed, so it is still impossible to give a detailed analysis of its architecture. By all appearances, however, it dates from the early years of the Empire. This is borne out by the simple construction of the vaults which, together with the side walls, are made of rubble. Only the center pillars and their linking arches are made of large blocks. The groined or quadripartite vault achieved by the cutting of two barrel vaults at right angles was unknown to the architect, who could otherwise have used this device at the intersections of the galleries. As it is, an L-shaped pillar stands at each corner; the vaults of the two galleries, set at right angles, rest on its outer faces, forming a sloping edge where they meet, which extends the height of the corner of the pillar.

This arrangement prepares the way for the quadripartite vault and is found for the first time in the Temple of Hercules at Tivoli, dating from the middle of the first century B.C.

The earliest example of a groined vault where the two sloped edges cut in a cross, appears in the house of the 'cryptoporticus' at Pompeii which was altered in the reign of Augustus. The 'cryptoportici' at Arles belong to the beginning of his reign; during the work of clearance a fine marble statue was discovered, showing him as a young man when he was still a triumvir known as Octavius Caesar.

The beauty of the galleries at Arles, like that of the Pont du Gard, derives solely from their powerful conception, their harmonious plan, and the quality of the materials used in their construction. It is also increased by their mysterious darkness contrasting with the sunlit landscape.

Archaeologists have argued inconclusively over the purpose of the galleries at Arles. The name of 'cryptoporticus' which has been accorded them is given to the long, shady corridors in Roman villas, designed for rest and walking in the heat of the day. The construction at Arles, however, must have been public and the large rectangle which it surrounds was, in all probability, the town forum; the great temple which dominated the square and divided the galleries with its foundations was most likely the Capitol. One theory is that they were storehouses for provisions, another that they really were public 'cryptoportici.'

The Oil Factory at Brisgane

Most Roman buildings designed for economic activity had a commercial function, and there are some surviving examples which can really be called factories. In this respect, too, Rome can be singled out from all other ancient and medieval civilizations, though the Romans were not the first to concentrate production in premises each employing several hundred workers. The 'tycoons' of the Hellenistic world had already realized similar undertakings, but no trace of them is left. Nor have many of the great Roman factories survived; industries connected with food are the only ones that have left traces, amongst them a flour-mill, using water wheels, dating from the fourth century A.D., excavated a few years ago at Barbegal in Provence.

The most impressive ruins are those of the oil factories on the African plateaux. These stand in a now practically deserted landscape, but one which, between the second and tenth centuries A.D., maintained quite a sizeable population thanks to the production of olive oil, extracted in huge factories. The main portion consists of rooms housing the presses, but the whole complex gains a monumental character due to a large courtyard with colonnades separating the work rooms from the warehouse where the olives and jars of oil were stored.

At the Brisgane factory, some twenty miles south of Tebessa, the soil is tawny-colored, and the ruin suggests a huge cage, the bars of which are formed of enormous blocks of limestone. This strange appearance is due to a highly remarkable constructional technique: small rubble was reinforced by large stone trusses set vertically, on top of which rested a horizontal course, again formed of big blocks. The corners of the building and the arches surrounding the courtyard were constructed of more large blocks. The arches support stone beams, cleverly arranged so that they do not rest on the keystones. They are either cut so that their ends rest on the headstones on either side of the keystone, or a single stone beam, equal in length to the diameter of the arch, is used. This is raised a few inches above the arch by blocks resting on the supporting pillars, embedded in grooves cut in the upper surface of the headstones. Relying, with justification, on the solidity of this framework, the country masons were less insistent than their city colleagues on the quality of the mortar. This has frequently resulted in weather completely wearing away the rubble filling and leaving untouched the stone courses, giving the peculiar cage-like appearance.

The history of this technical process is very interesting. The Carthaginians were the first to reinforce rubble with stone uprights between which ran binding stones attached to the rubble. The technique was borrowed by their conquerors during the Punic Wars, and examples of it may be found at Pompeii. Later on, it was abandoned in Italy because of the advance of the 'opus caementicium,' but it survived in the country of its origin right up to the end of antiquity and was even used in monumental architecture there at the height of the Empire.

The example at Brisgane shows that builders in these southernmost regions thought of using it to ensure a balance of forces which the architects of Rome achieved with the help of more sophisticated methods. The oil factories of the African plateaux are also of great interest to historians of the Empire. They prove that concentrated manufacture of certain products found an easy market. Rome, for example, with more than one million inhabitants, would have been threatened with starvation had it not been for the efforts of a large merchant fleet to support the city.

The Horrea Epagathiana at Ostia

One of the chief concerns of the Emperors of the first and second centuries was to ensure a regular food supply on which the public depended. Work on a vast scale was necessary to create an adequate harbor at Ostia: the docks were begun by Claudius (41-53) and doubled in size in Trajan's reign, following a new scheme which

Ostia: Trajan's harbor. About 1:2000.

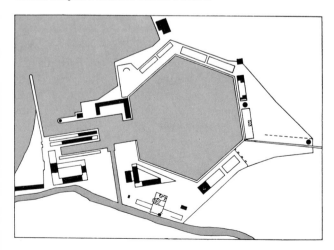

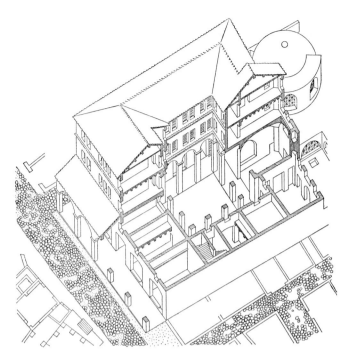

Ostia: axonometric view of an island block, the 'Casa dei Serapide' (after Kähler).

finally resulted in the building of a new town, Portus Traiani, later Porto. These built-up areas embodied the most characteristic and up-to-date aspects of Imperial civilization. Living accommodation was arranged in large tenement blocks, each with several floors and numerous flats. A large portion of the area was occupied by docks and warehouses. The architects had also devized a type of building that could be used as a private dwelling as well as the headquarters of a business organization, or even a barracks. A good example is the building erected about the middle of the second century A.D. by Epagathus and Epaphrodite, two freedmen from the East, to house the large import business which they owned. The 'Horrea Epagathiana' takes the form of a large rectangular building of three storeys, built entirely of brick. Pilasters divide the first floor façade into six equal sections, the second of which, starting from the large arch, is taken up by the door which is not set on the axis of the building as is usual in Roman architecture. This entrance is perfectly preserved and monumental in character; the great arch leading to the vestibule is framed by two engaged columns made of brick, with stucco capitals supporting an entablature and pediment. The dedicatory inscription, carved in marble, is set in the center of the frieze. Each of the remaining five sections was occupied by a shop with a wide rectangular opening under a depressed relieving arch; higher up, above the pilasters, another row of relieving arches forms a frame for small, square windows, and, finally, the second floor is crowned by a narrow, ornamental balcony. On the restored upper floors are pairs of windows which form a regular rhythm. Through the vestibule is a large rectangular courtyard surrounded by high brick arches leading into a covered walk.

The remarkable feature of this utilitarian building is not so much its monumentality as the refinement of its decoration. Its aesthetic elegance, ingenious yet unostentatious, resulted from a development in taste. We have seen, in the Pont du Gard and the Crytoportici at Arles, that Roman utilitarian buildings of the first century derived their beauty wholly from their powerful scale. The architect of Ostia, however, has also made use of effects of form and color which his Italian successors were to continue to employ to good advantage throughout the Middle Ages and in modern times. The master architect who directed his art towards these fresh paths was Apollodorus of Damascus, who built the great markets of the Quirinal for Trajan.

Trajan's Markets

Trajan's Markets form part of a still larger plan. The plunder taken from the Dacians made good the deficit which had endangered the finances of the Empire in Domitian's reign, and allowed Trajan to complete the monumental plan for the center of Rome, begun a hundred and fifty years earlier by Julius Caesar. The dictator had created a square parallel to the old Forum Romanum and to the north-east were successively added the Forum of Augustus, the Forum Transitorium and the huge precinct of the Temple of Peace built by the Flavians. Trajan's work equalled in importance all that of his predecessors put together. From east to west, it consisted of the Forum Traiani, the Basilica Ulpia, the two libraries flanking the famous column that still survives, and the area on which, after his death, his successor Hadrian erected a temple dedicated to his memory.

The Markets dominated the Forum from the slopes of the Quirinal which had been quarried out to the height of one hundred feet to accommodate the vast construction. Its highly original plan was completely different from that of the 'macellae' in provincial towns, usually consisting of rectangular squares surrounded by shops. The arrangement of the Markets was dictated by the slope of the ground and the need to establish a link with the Forum.

Apollodorus could have followed the tradition of his predecessors by dividing the slope into tiers and setting rectangular buildings on them. Instead, he planned his buildings round a large semicircle which formed a buttress for the hill

Ostia: façade of the Horrea Epagathiana.
About 1:400

53

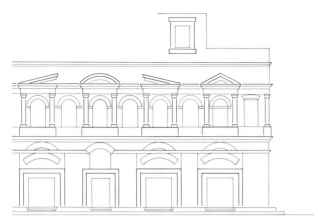

Rome: façade of Trajan's Markets, section of the hemicycle. About 1:400.

which he had quarried away. This also enabled an apse to be placed within the curve which widened the square and was repreated on the south side facing Caesar's Forum. These two great semicircles resemble the ones terminating the Forum of Augustus, and surrounding the two apses of the Basilica Ulpia, both of which have the same radius. The hemicycle of the Market has a concave façade with two tiers of arches. A semicircular gallery had already made an appearance in the early first century B.C. in the Temple of Fortune at Praeneste, one of the

Trajan's Markets: section of shops and the Via Biberatica.

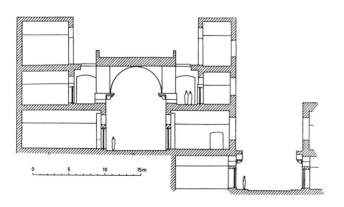

first purely Roman monuments; but this consisted of a colonnaded portico.

Apollodorus' concave façade was in fact similar to the convex ones produced by the builders of theaters and amphitheaters. The first-floor arches house the rectangular surrounds of luxury shops and those above serve as windows lighting a promenade which gives access to a second set of shops. The upper arches are framed by pilasters and an entablature following the scheme first realized on the Tabularium on a straight façade, and also used in theater buildings with a convex plan. It is necessary to stress the importance of this innovation and its architectural connections, including all buildings designed for public shows and many triumphal and funerary monuments or purely decorative features such as fountains. Here we find a meeting place for the two mainstreams dominating Imperial architecture: the functional tendency whose development has been outlined previously, and the baroque. Henceforward these two streams are no longer in opposition, but complementary and united against classicism.

The baroque characteristic of Apollodorus' façade stems primarily from its outline and the fact that its two halves are dissimilar—though at a first glance they seem identical. Moreover, it is stressed by the color contrasts between the background of red brick, the basic constructional material, and the white travertine framing the shops which were paved with mosaic; their walls were also covered with frescoes. The striking richness of the Horrea Epagathiana at Ostia may well have been inspired by Trajan's building. Another baroque effect was obtained from the rhythm of the pediments crowning the third-floor arches. They were either shaped like isosceles triangles in the usual way or divided into right-angled triangles. It is of great interest to confirm that this upper storey was never masked by medieval buildings and was often sketched by lovers of ruins in the sixteenth century.

At the eastern end of Apollodorus' semicircle is the entrance to an ancient street still preserved in modern Rome. This is the Via Biberatica, which rises above the hemicycle, serving the maze of shops which are backed by the hill. It winds round the flank of the Quirinal after the fashion of the 'clivi' of ancient Rome, which later townplanners so often replaced by terraces linked by steps. This street is bordered by shops similar to those of the Horrea Epagathiana, with travertine surrounds surmounted by relieving arches and a balcony above, and plays a part in the composition similar to the passage ('praecinctio') dividing the tiers of a Roman theater. On the upper level two sets of buildings radiate from the curve, one to the north, the other to the east. The former is more important and has for its axis a huge rectangular nave covered by six adjacent groined vaults—the Basilica of Trajan.

Amphitheaters: El Djem

The connections just noted between the plans of Trajan's Markets and those of theaters lead us to an examination of buildings designed for public entertainment—in this case not the Colosseum or the arenas of Provence, but the little known amphitheater of El Djem in Tunisia.

El Djem today is a town of a few thousand inhabitants, on the east coast of Tunisia. From the long, straight road linking it with Sousse, there is a sudden view of a vast ochre-colored cylinder rising high above the gray olive trees and low white houses: closer to, it appears to be pierced by regularly spaced black holes. The vast building blots out the village, and it seems amazing that so gigantic a structure should have been erected for the entertainment of the

forerunners of the Bedouins who now hold their market beneath its arches. This is not so amazing, however, now that excavations organised by the National Archeological Institute of Tunisia have revealed a large network of streets bordered by luxurious villas beyond the boundaries of the modern town.

In the second and third centuries, Thysdrus, the ancient El Djem, was a center of the oil industry, taking precedence over Sbeitla, Kairoun and Sfax. It was during this period of affluence, probably about 200, that they built this African Colosseum to replace the old arenas which were hewn out of the earth and have now been once more revealed.

An amphitheater, as its name suggests, is a theater in the round, completely self-contained. In Rome the defenders of the ancient codes of behavior did not permit the construction of a permanent theater until the middle of the first century B.C., and even then it needed all Pompey's prestige as conqueror of the East to bring it about. The site chosen was the Campus Martius where the common people had long held their fairs. It was the only area in this hilly city which was completely level and, it was therefore, impossible to hollow out steps, though the earth could have been built up into artificial ones. This simple and economical solution was adopted in some small towns, such as Ventimiglia on the Genoese riviera, and at Leptis; but in Pompey's day, architects had just discovered the manifold possibilities of vaults and curvilinear architecture. So they had the idea of raising their steps on a series of superimposed arches which presented a semicircular outer façade. In this way the Roman theater came into being.

After the invention of theaters built on arches, the same principle was applied to amphitheaters. The arenas of southern France, including the perfectly preserved specimens at Arles and Nîmes, must be among the oldest examples, though their dates cannot be precisely fixed. Indeed, it was not until the construction of the Colosseum by the Flavian Emperors and its dedication in 80 A.D., that provincial architects had an example that could be universally imitated.

The amphitheater at Thysdrus was an imita-

Plan of the Flavian Amphitheater, or Colosseum. About 1:1000.

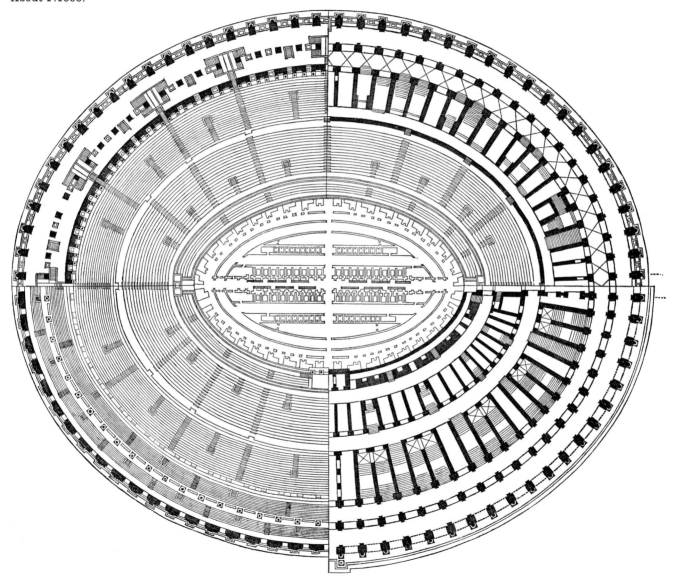

tion of the Colosseum at Rome, built over a century previously. Nevertheless, it differs greatly in appearance. The series of piers has been replaced by what is really a solid wall whose unity is unbroken by the high, narrow arches and the engaged columns framing them. This impressive sense of mass is due wholly to technical reasons. The Colosseum is built of travertine, and the Gallic arenas of solid limestone, both highly resistant materials allowing a reduction of the surface forming the points of support. The Tunisian Sahel, on the other hand, is so badly off for building stone that the most luxurious houses of Thysdrus and the neighboring towns are often constructed of rough bricks. The architect of the amphitheater had to be content with sandstone, the softness of which forced him to make his piers wider. With its almost completely ruined attic, which seems never to have been completed, the amphitheater at El Djem has the look of a fortress and, indeed, played the part of one very effectively after the fall of the Empire.

At El Djem the arrangement of the promenades is inseparable from the façade. Every amphitheater had these huge galleries circling the building; at regular intervals they were joined by the vaulted passageways leading from the ellipse of the arena, the upper surfaces of their arches forming supports for the tiers of seats. The outer promenade of the Colosseum is roofed with a continuous barrel vault. At Thysdrus the piers of the promenade are linked by transverse arches and the passageway is roofed with a series of barrel vaults at right angles to the façade, each corresponding to one of the arches. In this way the outer wall receives no thrust.

The Italian architects of the Seicento and Settecento were directly influenced by amphitheater façades. Alberti, for instance, used the architrave supported by consoles, which crowned

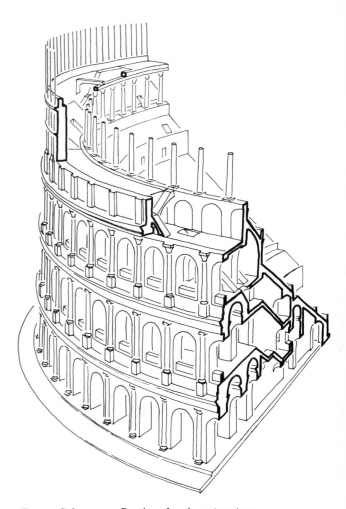

Rome: Colosseum. Section showing structure.

the attic of the Colosseum, in the Palazzo Ruccellai in Florence. The Romans, too, as we shall see, adapted the system of superimposed arches to more complex monumental façades.

The Porta Nigra at Trier

The Porta Nigra forms a monumental entrance to the city of Trier which, in the second and third centuries, was an extremely important economic center, and, in the fourth century, became the political and military headquarters of the Emperor of the West. Its plan reverts to a prototype used since Hellenistic times. The actual gate is composed of thin arches and flanked by two semicircular towers from which the defenders could engage their attackers. The architect, however, has endowed this simple lay-out with a remarkable extension, both in plan and elevation. Instead of leading directly into the town, the double gateway emerges into a square courtyard the sides of which are formed by the prolongations of the towers; it is closed by a second façade parallel to the first. These two façades each rise to three storeys and the towers to four. Thus, from outside, the Porta Nigra's silhouette resembles that of a Romanesque cathedral with twin towers, though it does not form a compact mass like a church: the yawning darkness of its many windows gives it an air of romantic mystery. At each level the façade forms a loggia of six small arcades flanked by sturdy engaged columns which project on pilasters. Their capitals are Corinthian, but the baskets lack their ornamental foliage so that the order takes on an almost Doric vigor. Similar arches with identical framing stand out in the massive towers. Here again is the prin-ciple of the façade of the Tabularium dating from Sulla's time, completed and developed by the circular movement of the towers. This formula was widely used in the late third and fourth centuries A.D. for the palaces of Emper-ors or noblemen, which already appeared quite feudal.

The palace at Split, to which Diocletian retired after his abdication, is surrounded on three sides by a massive curtain-wall; the fourth, facing the sea, is composed of a podium surmounted by a huge loggia with rectangular towers at each end.

The Porta Nigra marks a transition between two types of Roman architecture of the classic period and other styles already belonging to the Middle Ages. There is, however, no evidence for an exact dating, which has given rise to lively debates between holders of opposing theories. Some say that it goes back to the late first century A.D., while others maintain that it is no earlier than the fourth century, when the city was an Imperial residence.

Roman Military Architecture

A large number of military works bear witness to the importance of this type of construction in Roman architecture and, while the Porta Nigra may be one of the last wholly Roman creations, it was preceded by a series of earlier fortifica-tions. The most ancient piece of military archi-tecture to have left some surviving traces is the

Trier: Porta Nigra, reconstruction.

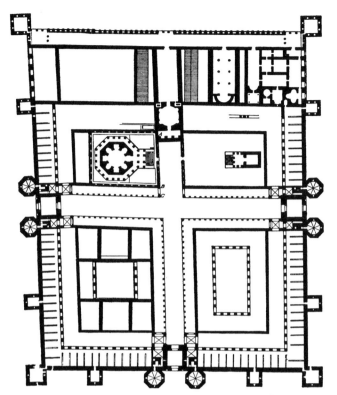

Split (Spalato): plan of Diocletian's Palace. About 1:2000.

station. It was composed of a wide terrace, supported on the outer side by a wall of tufa from Grotta Ferrata, nearly 33 feet high and 12 feet wide at the base; in front of this curtain-wall was a ditch, nearly 99 feet wide and 29 feet deep. This defence system was comparable to the most notable Hellenistic fortifications and assured the city every protection; Hannibal had good reason for refusing to attack it.

In the second half of the fourth century, Rome began to establish colonies throughout Italy: these were basically military posts ('castra'), small towns, square or rectangular in plan, surrounded by a rampart with four gates sited in the middle of each side, which was linked by two straight main streets running at right angles to one another. Ostia, which was founded in 338 B.C. formed a rectangle, 636 feet by 412 feet. This type of fortress-camp or 'castrum' was closely related to the ordinary military camp which was known by the same name. According to Polybius in the mid-second century B.C., these were really temporary towns with walls on the same principle as those of Rome—a terrace, or 'agger' surmounted by a parapet and fronted by a ditch—axial gateways, streets, and a central square. The problem is whether this was a genuinely Roman conception or one borrowed from an earlier age.

Frontinus asserts beyond a shadow of doubt that his countrymen learned the rules of camp construction from a survey of the camp of Pyrrhus, King of Epirus, after the victorious battle of Beneventum in 275 B.C. If this information is true, Roman camps must have been inspired by Hellenistic town-planning, just as the fortifications of Rome must have been largely owing to the skill of Greek military engineers from the West introduced by the Etruscans.

There was little development in the principles

city wall of Rome. There are still several points between the Palatine, the Capitol, and the Esquiline where it is possible to see the remains of a rampart built of small blocks of rock known as 'cappelaccio.' Archaeologists are unanimous in agreeing that this wall which was eventually nearly 4½ miles round, dates from the sixth century, thus justifying the tradition, wrongly discredited in the nineteenth century, that the fortification was the work of the Etruscan king, Servius Tullius.

After the invasion of the Gauls early in the fourth century, this wall was reinforced by a second, traces of which may still be seen between the Quirinal and the Esquiline, particularly in the vicinity of the present railway of Roman fortifications during the three centuries preceding the Christian era; and, at the beginning of the Empire, camps were still organized in more or less the same manner as in the days of Polybius. The one set up by Drusus at Haltern in Westphalia was only occupied for a few years at the very end of the first century B.C., until its evacuation after the revolt of Arminius in 8 A.D., and offers an excellent example of this type of fortification completely fashioned of wood and stone.

The stabilization of the frontier dating from the reign of Augustus gradually resulted in the creation of a line of permanent fortifications, known as the 'Limes.' This term really applied to the road following the frontier line, linking a series of camps and fortified posts. These camps were meant for the garrison troops and the chief ones were occupied by a legion. The best known example is the camp of Lambaesis in the south of the province of Constantine,which was built in the reign of Hadrian (117-138) and was the headquarters of the 3rd Augustan legion, the core of the army of Africa. In its general lines, the plan still conforms to the pattern quoted by Polybius, but buildings and fortifications were constructed of stone. The most interesting architectural feature is the 'principia' or 'praetorium,' the headquarter buildings, placed in the center where the main thoroughfares meet, the usual site of forum and capitol in a city plan.

A monumental entrance in the form of a triumphal arch leads to a vast courtyard lined on three sides by colonnades, behind which lies a series of small similar rooms used as administrative offices or storehouses. On the fourth side, facing the entrance, is a raised, rectangular space. At its far end, behind a colonnade, stretches a series of apsidal rooms, the center one of which was the most important, serving as the sanctuary of the divinities of the legion. Among them was the eagle, the legion's emblem, which was considered a divinity.

In European camps this raised area, which is uncovered at Lambaesis, was provided with a roof and so resembled a basilica. This combination has been compared with that of the square and basilica in Trajan's Forum and in many provincial fora. A theory has even been advanced that this type of civic center may have been inspired by military buildings, but this has never been proved.

In regions where the frontier did not depend on natural defences such as a great river, a mountain range, or an expanse of desert, the Romans built a continuous rampart to prevent the passage of the barbarians. The best known example is the wall built by Hadrian from the mouth of the Solway to the Tyne.

Because their security was assured in this way, the Romans of the Empire did not, as a rule, deem it worthwhile maintaining city walls. Very often, as in Gaul, strongholds on hills were abandoned in favor of sites on the plains where the built-up areas expanded freely. Fortified gateways were replaced by decorative entrances, often in the form of triumphal arches, as at Orange. A few towns situated in troubled areas kept their ramparts: Cherchel, in Algeria, is a specially interesting example of a fortified town of the Middle Empire.

In the middle of the third century, the Augustan military system which had already been jeopardized by the invasion of the Quadi and Marcommani in 169 A.D., collapsed completely. Barbarian invasions of the Empire were now constant, and the legionaries yielded their pride of place in battle to the cavalry. The direct result of this was the reappearance of the fortified town. No sign of this has been found in Africa, the East, or in Provence. Nevertheless, many walls were built and, in 272 A.D., Aurelian decided to protect Rome in this way.

Most of the towns of Gallia Comata had been destroyed during the great invasions of the mid-third century, and were replaced, at the beginning of the tetrarchy, by strongpoints which were again given the old name of 'castra.' In some cases, including Strasbourg, they were the camps of the Middle Empire restored, and the civil population continued to live outside, with the option of taking refuge within the ramparts as soon as danger threatened. Usually the fortifications surrounded the urban center of the old settlement, as at Dijon; the walls were sometimes roughly rectangular as at Dijon and Bordeaux, sometimes circular, as at Grenoble, Sens and Rennes. Their length was not very great. All these walls are uniform in construction, showing that they were designed according to a master plan and to the orders of high authority. Their foundations are massive, yet not very deep, and are usually formed of second-hand materials from ruined buildings of the Middle Empire.

Army reform led to a radical transformation of large and small forts. The camp in miniature was replaced by a type of building in which all the basic elements of a fortified castle were already visible. It consisted of a redoubt standing in the center of a curtain-wall which surrounded a square courtyard. These 'castella' were designed for the use of the peasant militia who

Rome: crenellated wall and towers of the Praetorian Camp.

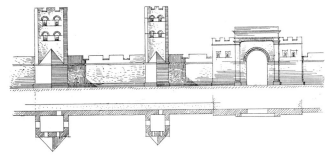

from now on had the task of covering the front line of the frontier. Their courtyards were ready to receive the families and cattle of the frontier dwellers at the approach of the enemy. In Africa, at the beginning of the fourth century, there was a great increase in the number of forts. A special feature is the distribution of barrack buildings along the inner side of the ramparts. In Gaul, the 'castellum' of Jublains in Mayenne is smaller than an African 'centenarium,' but resembles them with its corner towers and bastions. Along the Syrian frontier, at Qdeym and Amsareddi near Chalcis, are 'centenaria' exactly like those in Africa, which proves that this type of fortress must have been built according to plans drawn up by the Imperial High Command.

Chief Characteristics

The buildings discussed in this chapter are all perfect illustrations of the individual genius of Roman architecture. Each one has an essentially practical aim, either commercial or military. This even includes the amphitheaters, as gladiatorial combats were regarded as miniature wars sustaining the martial qualities of a victorious nation. The army exercised strict control over the economy, the civil service being no more than an extension of the military organization which was administered according to the same principles. Labor forces from the legions and skilled military engineers were used in the construction of the aqueducts. Thus the nation which prided itself on its descent from Mars considered all its basic activities as complementary extensions of war. Its merit lies in having directed virtues primarily used for defence and the conquest of its neighbors further and further towards constructive undertakings. This development may be followed in all branches of culture, and particularly in literature. In the art of building, as we have seen, it produced a highly bold and original form of aesthetic which made no concessions to frivolous decoration.

All buildings had as their aim the welfare of the public. Everyone—apart from rebels who were pitilessly crushed—from the Emperor down to the meanest slave, could find a place within them and his own share of the common good. The overwhelming strength of the Empire was meant for protection, not oppression.

Plates

El-Djem (formerly Thysdrus), Tunisia: Amphitheater

67 Interior promenade of the amphitheater at El-Djem, one of the largest and best preserved of the Roman world.

68 The amphitheater dominates the present village and dates from the beginning of the third century A.D.

69 Detail of the façade. The width of the spaces separating the arches gives the monument a massive appearance.

70 The arena, beneath which lie two galleries shaped like a cross. These were lined by vaulted chambers containing cages for wild animals.

71 The auditorium, from the bottom of one of the subterranean galleries.

Trier: Porta Nigra

72 Outer façade. The plan was borrowed from Hellenistic military architecture.

73 Façade to the town. The decoration is reduced to a minimum.

74 Interior court separating the two façades. The decoration of the upper order is not antique.

Nîmes: Maison Carrée

75 Façade and pronaos. This is the best preserved of all the classic Augustan temples.

76 Side view. The temple is pseudo-peripteral (the columns, apart from those of the pronaos, are engaged in the cella wall). This is a Roman formula which made its appearance in the 2nd century B.C.

77 Detail of the classic Roman Corinthian order. One of the earliest examples of this type.

78 Detail of one of the Attic bases. A single concave, or scotia, molding separates two torus mouldings.

Nîmes: "Temple of Diana"

79 General view of the interior. The roof consists of a barrel vault formed of large blocks with ribs corresponding to the strong points of the wall, between the niches.

80 a, b. Detail of the pediments of the niches.

81 One of the longer side walls. The decoration of baroque inspiration is similar to that of theater stages.

82 In the foreground, the pillars of the aedicule which probably housed a statue of the cult. In the background, the niches and entablature of one of the side walls.

Baalbek (Lebanon): Temple of Bacchus

83 General view of the exterior of the cella.

84 The outer colonnade.

85 Detail of capitals and architrave, and the pediment of one of the niches of the upper order.

86 The door and interior of the cella. In the background, the adyton. On the right, baroque decoration of the wall with sham colonnade.

87 Detail of door surround. The baroque decoration is deeply incised, leaving no plain surface.

88 The adyton and decoration of one of the side walls.

89 Pedestal supporting a column with an Attic base.

Rome: The Pantheon

90 The pronaos, showing the powerful severity of the giant order with decoration reduced to an absolute minimum. The inscription with Agrippa's name recalls an earlier temple demolished to make way for Hadrian's.

91 Interior of the rotunda. The lower storey is antique, the second was reconstructed in the seventeenth century.

92 Detail of the interior order.

93 The dome with its coffered decoration and circular roof open, the only source of lighting, has remained unaltered since the reign of Septimius Severus.

94 Detail of the coffers on the dome.

La **Porta Nigra:**
coupe, élévation et plan 1:400

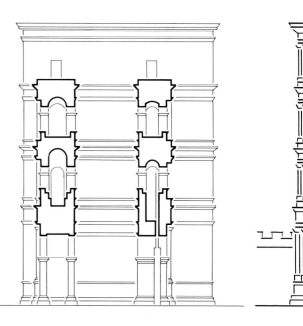

Trier Plan of the Roman town 1:30000.
    A. Imperial Thermae
    B. Porta Nigra

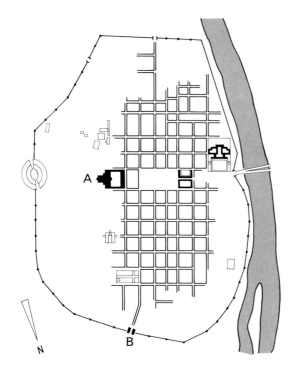

Porta Nigra Section, elevation and plan. 1:400.

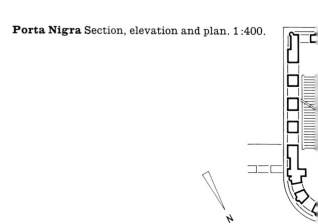

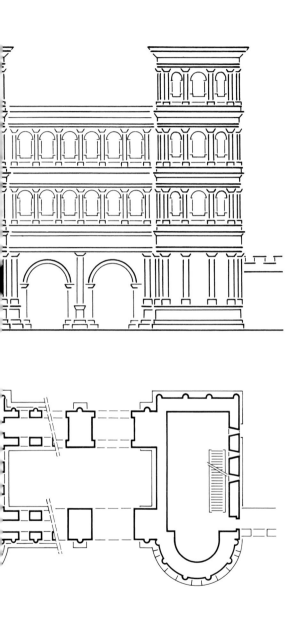

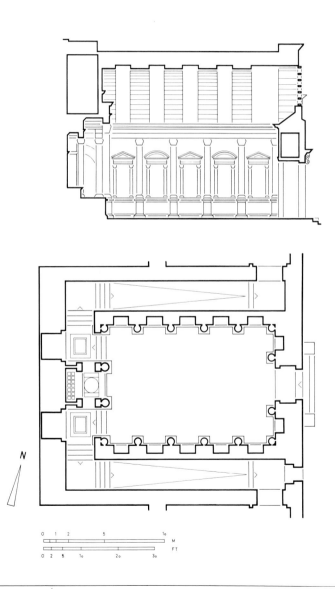

Temple of Diana at Nîmes Longitudinal section and plan 1:300.

N

0 1 2   5   10   M
                                        FT
0 2 5   10   20   30

Notes

Nîmes

Towards the end of the 3rd century B.C., a powerful Celtic tribe, the Volcae Arecomici, settled on the Mediterranean border of the Massif Central. A freely flowing spring issuing from the foot of a steep hill in the Garrigues was personified as the god Nemausus whose cult was practised on the summit of the hill, on the site of the Tour Magne. The tribe's political center was set up near these sacred places. The Volcae became subject to Rome at the end of the second century B.C., but it was not until a century later, in the reign of Augustus, that a colony of veterans was established in the town. Some of them had served in Egypt, hence the palm tree and crocodile still incorporated in the town's crest. In 16 B.C., Nîmes was given a fortified wall including the Gate of Augustus and also incorporating the Tour Magne. The sanctuary of the spring was made into a nymphaeum later completed by the so-called Temple of Diana. The civic center consisted of the forum which, as usual, occupied the center of the planned area. This square was dominated by the temple of the Maison Carrée, built not later than 12 B.C.: its original dedication was probably to the Imperial cult.

Baalbek

Syria, in the Imperial period, was one of the liveliest parts of the Empire. The country owed its wealth partly to agriculture, partly to the manufacture of luxury goods, but above all to trade. It played the part of intermediary between the Mediterranean world and Asia, which included not only Iranian Asia, its immediate neighbor, but also the Chinese Far East, by virtue of the silk trade. It formed a meeting place for a great variety of nations and civilizations. Three elements played an essential part in this. First, the Semites, who formed the backbone of the population: they maintained their traditions, especially in the sphere of religion, and their language underwent a brilliant revival from the 3rd century A.D. onwards. The Greeks settled in the country in large numbers after the conquest of Alexander, imposing on it their culture, language, and political institutions. Finally the Romans came to govern, with their military and administrative genius.

Baalbek (in Greek, Heliopolis), the city of the sun, is therefore an example of an ancient sacerdotal city where Augustus established a group of Roman colonists. This conjunction did little to modify the character of the city whose life, like that of many other Asian towns, revolved round its temples, thus differing fundamentally from purely Roman cities whose religious functions tended to diminish and became popularized. The building of the religious center became the main preoccupation of the community over several centuries. The principal temple dates from the mid-first century A.D. The great colonnaded forecourt with its altar towers was completed in the first half of the second century and was immediately followed by the construction of the small temple which is better preserved, as may be seen from the illustrations. The Bacchic decoration of this sanctuary sets a difficult problem for historians of religion. The neighboring round temple, one of the most remarkable baroque buildings of antiquity, was reconstructed in the mid-third century, while the hexagonal vestibule preceding the great court and the propylaea completing it, were contributed in the Severan period. Baalbek is one of the Syrian sites where architecture is most strongly marked by purely Roman influence, though the underlying spirit of the work reveals itself as very different from that of the monumental buildings of the West.

Julius Lacer

Beside the great architects employed by the Emperors there were more modest craftsmen working in the provinces: amongst them, that of Julius Lacer is of particular interest. This Spanish architect built a fine bridge over the Tagus in Trajan's reign: it still survives and has given the nearby town its name of Alcantara—the Arabic for "bridge". Built in 103-104 A.D. it was paid for by eleven cities of Lusitania whose names are carved, below a dedication to the Emperor, on a triumphal arch which stands in the center of the span. Lacer also built a smaller temple on the river bank. An approximate translation of its dedication, recorded in the sixteenth century, reads:

"Who has given this temple on the rock of the Tagus inhabited by the gods and Caesar, a work of art overcoming matter itself, and by virtue of what vow? Travellers helped by this new glory will perhaps be anxious to know. It is Lacer who has realized this huge bridge with its massive bulk, who has accomplished the rites of a sacrifice pleasing to the gods. Lacer, ennobled by a divine art, built this bridge which should survive over all the centuries of the world's existence. This same Lacer who made the bridge and dedicated new temples—doubtless such gifts please the gods—also erected a temple for the gods of Romulus and for Caesar. Happy cause of these two sacrifices!"

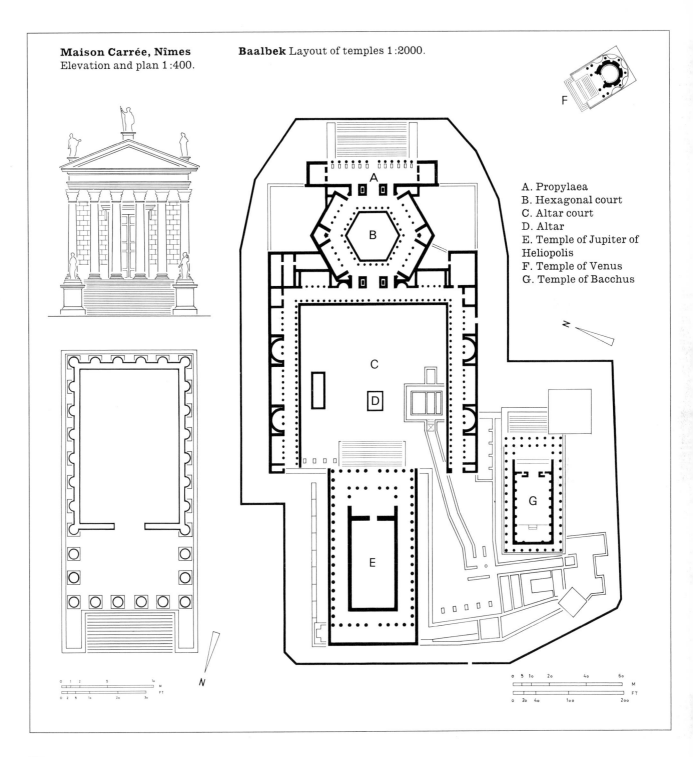

Maison Carrée, Nîmes
Elevation and plan 1 :400.

Baalbek Layout of temples 1 :2000.

A. Propylaea
B. Hexagonal court
C. Altar court
D. Altar
E. Temple of Jupiter of
Heliopolis
F. Temple of Venus
G. Temple of Bacchus

Temple of Bacchus, Baalbek Transverse section
and plan 1:600, longitudinal section, 1:400.

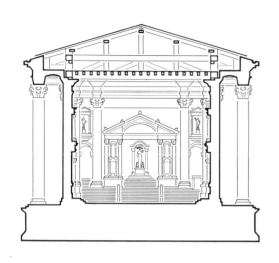

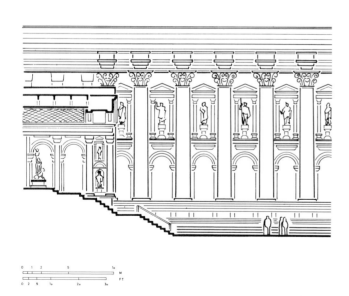

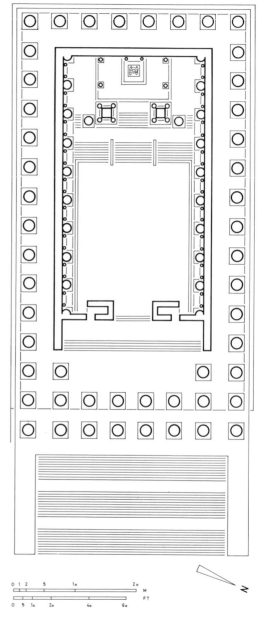

3. From Classicism to Baroque

The rough, military aspect of Roman civilization with its expression of strength, discussed in the previous chapter, was very soon put to the service of a spiritual ideal. This we know from personal contact gained through the surviving writings of individual Romans. Rome became the champion of Greek civilization, which it both adopted and adapted to its own requirements, a fact so well known that it may seem too commonplace to stress. On the other hand, there has for long been a belief that, at any rate in the domain of art, Rome did no more than copy Hellenism, rendering it lifeless and degraded.

The essential individuality of Roman art was only revealed when, due to the progress of archaeological techniques, historians were able to consider complete schemes instead of isolated components. Not until then did they realize the close connection of sculptors with painters, and their joint subordination to the architect. Then it was possible to show that the Romans, while thriving on their Greek heritage, completely reworked it. Outside the sphere of functional architecture, the aesthetic value of which had also been misunderstood, the art of the Empire often found expression in forms strangely similar to those of seventeenth and eighteenth century Baroque. The continual attention paid by the architects of these two centuries to antique monuments is sufficient explanation of a relationship that is by no means accidental. Not all Imperial architecture may be termed Baroque, however. Classical tendencies prevailed at certain periods, particularly at the start of the Christian era, and, though this is not the only time worthy of note, it should no longer be neglected. It is evident that this Roman classicism was no more a mechanical repetition of the art of Phidias than French classicism of the Louis XIV period was of either.

In this chapter the originality and perfection of Augustan architecture will be demonstrated by an examination of the best known architectural monuments. There follows an attempt to trace the logical movement from Classicism to Baroque which turned these opposing tendencies into complementary expressions of the Roman character.

The Maison Carrée at Nîmes

After Augustus put an end to the civil wars, he turned his attention to re-establishing the nation's religious life, starting with a restoration of the sanctuaries which had fallen in to ruin. Unfortunately nothing remains of the Temple of Apollo Palatinus, built to commemorate Actium, apart from a levelled podium. The walls of the huge Temple of Mars Ultor still rise above the Forum of Augustus and have now been freed from the modern buildings surrounding them, but the superstructure and most of the colonnades have disappeared. On the other hand, three columns of the Temple of Apollo near the Theater of Marcellus have been rediscovered: these soar skywards in isolation, giving some idea of the building's pristine elegance.

But for a real appreciation of Augustan religious architecture we must go to Provence. Here there are many ruined sanctuaries, some of great charm like the one buried in a green valley at Vernègues, others transmitting a feeling of power, despite their small dimensions, like the chapel of the Santé at Saint-Rémy. Two temples in France which are practically intact may well claim to be the most famous antique survivals in the world: the Temple of Augustus and Livia at Vienne, and the Maison Carrée at Nîmes in Provence.

Recent research has enabled us to appreciate the originality of the Maison Carrée, a perfect masterpiece of Roman classicism. The temple was commissioned by Agrippa and can therefore be dated before his death in 12 B.C., as is shown by the dedicatory inscription of bronze letters originally fixed to the frieze of the façade, which can still be made out from the nail holes in which the letters were fixed. Kähler has proved that the building was the work of a team of architects responsible for the chief temples in Rome between 20 and 10 B.C. They used the rules of classic Greek architecture and pursued the same ideal without copying past examples.

The originality of the Maison Carrée lies in the temple that was the key feature of its architectural setting. This was rediscovered during excavations carried out at the time of the Restoration, but has now been covered over by the modern town. It was basically composed of the town forum, a rectangular square more than 262 feet long, surrounded by colonnades. The southern section, the center of which was occupied by the temple, was raised $3\frac{1}{2}$ feet above the area of the square itself. The colonnades surrounding the three sides of the forum also had their floors level with this esplanade throughout their length, so that they dominated the pavement of the square. The 'cella' of the temple almost touched the fourth side which had no colonnade and formed a shallow apse behind it.

The conception of a temple enclosed in a monumental surround originated in the architecture of Greece and in lands further east. The idea of the 'temenos,' the domain of the god extending beyond his house, was particularly exploited in the Hellenistic period. When the Romans took it up again, they gave it a special significance, making a combination of 'temenos' and 'agora' which resulted in the forum. The idea was elaborated in southern Italy during the centuries preceding the Christian era. Pompeii has one of the oldest examples of a rectangular forum dominated by a Capitol which rises at one end. Despite its regular plan, this square was not created as a unity: each successive civilization in the city from the fourth to the first century B.C. contributed its individual elaboration. During this same period the Forum at Rome offered the confused appearance which Sulla started to rearrange. It was left to Julius Caesar, however, to be the first to realize the formula later adopted by the colonists at Nîmes: a rectangular space, completely shut off by colonnades, surrounding a solitary temple dedicated to the cult of the dynasty, backing on to the small side facing the entrance. This placing of the shrine is a basic feature distinguishing an Italian forum from a Hellenistic 'temenos' where the temple was isolated in the center of the sacred area. In this way the Roman 'aedes' was more completely integrated in its setting.

The architect at Nîmes also introduced a highly individual innovation into this scheme: the raised esplanade at the back of the forum incorporating the podium of the temple which dominated it, and prolonged to include the lateral colonnades. In this way he created a stepped composition, completely in accordance with the spirit of the times, but usually only found in towns where there were natural differences of levels. The earliest example is Palestrina, and it occurs again, contemporary with Nîmes, at Carthage. The temple was set off to greater advantage, but the sharp changes in level must have resulted in practical inconveniences which explains why the idea was not repeated except where the lie of the ground dictated it.

The Maison Carrée on its esplanade was raised up nearly 10 feet more by a podium, a high platform borrowed by the Romans from the Etruscans. Entrance to the building, as in all Latin temples, is by means of steps set on the main front. The temple itself is pseudo-peripteral: the 'cella' has the columns of the rear façade and eight out of the eleven columns on each side set in its walls. In other words, the building can be divided into two clearly opposing sections: a deep, open portico and a massive, closed chamber. The peripteral design was unknown to the Greeks and made its appearance in Italy in the second half of the second century B.C. This plan came into being for practical reasons, including the desire to make the 'cella' as spacious as possible. It derived from another earlier typically Italian design, examples of which have also survived: the semi-peripteral temple, surrounded by a colonnade on three sides, but with the fourth shut by a plain wall. In Italy sanctuaries are always orientated unlike those in Greece where the two shorter façades are both alike; even completely peripteral temples are only accessible from one side.

Roman Corinthian

The Maison Carrée uses the Corinthian order which, at the time of its construction, had only just attained its definitive shape. During the Republic the Romans sometimes used the Doric order and, more often, the Tuscan, which did not derive from the Doric, but developed parallel with it. They also, as in the temple in the Velabrum, used the Ionic which continued to be a favorite with Augustan architects. After the fashion of the Greek settlers in Italy they often combined a Doric frieze with an Ionic colonnade. The Corinthian order first appeared in Greece in the late fifth century B.C.; it was already more popular than its rivals by the first century B.C., but assumed many variations in rapid succession according to changes in fashion. The capitals of the late Republic, for instance, vary greatly in their proportions, and the foliage covering their baskets is at times highly naturalistic, at times geometrical and stiff. Classification of these forms provides good evidence for datings.

The political stability brought about by Augustus almost immediately produced a stabilization of forms, and from now on architects were subject to the rules codified by Vitruvius who wrote in the early years of the Empire. These were copied from Renaissance times right up to the late nineteenth century and produced the classic Corinthian order—to which we are now so accustomed that it is impossible to imagine that it was not always thus ordained. It is typified by three main features: an Attic type base, an acanthus leaf capital, and a cornice with modillions. All these may be found at the Maison Carrée.

Roman Corinthian (after a 19th century engraving).

The simple, elegant bases consist fundamentally of a square plinth and two rounded, convex torus moldings separated by a concave scotia molding. They may be easily distinguished from earlier bases like those of the temple in the Santé at Saint-Rémy, dating from 39 B.C. These have no plinths and the scotia is so deep and closed that it looks like a saw cut separating the torus moldings. The Roman Corinthian order allowed the Attic type base as well as the Ionic with its greater number of moldings. The former was preferred by Augustan architects.

The capital above the fluted shaft is formed of a basket—'calathos' in Greek—shaped like a reversed truncated cone. It stands on a circular molding known as an astragal and is topped by an abacus which supports the entablature. The basket is decorated with two wreaths of acanthus leaves. From the top of these on each side of the capital, two pairs of croziers emerge from a flower shaped like a horn—the 'cauliculus.' The more developed of these croziers, the volute, extends to the corner of the abacus and supports it; the other, the spiral, turns inwards to face its fellow directly opposite. The concave abacus curves inwards and is divided into two moldings: the lower one is ornamented with gadroons, the upper one with a row of egg-and-dart. In the middle of the abacus, a flower-shaped ornament projects sharply outwards.

The capitals of the Maison Carrée can easily be distinguished from earlier types, first of all by their proportions. The height of the basket corresponds to the diameter of its base, and the second acanthus wreath crosses the horizontal axis of the capital which previously bounded it.

The lower wreath and the area of the volutes have the same dimensions, whereas the middle wreath is lower. The acanthus itself is completely different from Greek models, which continued to be used when opportunity presented itself, in the eastern portion of the Empire in addition to the Italian acanthus of the Republican period. Each leaf is divided into five lobes set symmetrically on either side of the center: these have curved ends like olive leaves. This softened form of acanthus can immediately be distinguished from the hard, spiky type found at Glanum (Saint-Rémy), and at the temple in Vienne on the oldest capitals, those of the pilasters embedded in the 'cella.' In addition, capitals dating from the Republic usually have a thicker abacus without any decoration, and the large flower ornament at the junction of the basket and the abacus projects over both instead of being confined to the abacus, as in this case. It is not so easy, however, to distinguish the Maison Carrée capitals from those of later buildings, such as the Temple of Castor and Pollux at Rome (6 A.D.) and the arch at Orange built in the reign of Tiberius in 27 A.D. Their acanthus flowers no longer share the lively yet somewhat arid elegance of those at Nîmes.

The entablature is formed of an architrave, frieze, and cornice. The latter has to fulfil both a decorative and a utilitarian function. Its duty is to shield the building from the rain and, for this reason, its upper portion is provided with a projection appropriately known as a dripstone. In the Greek Ionic and Corinthian orders this is supported by denticles formed by making regularly spaced rectangular gaps in a wide fillet. Roman architects at the beginning of the reign of Augustus had the idea of increasing the height and projection of the cornice by placing above the denticles a porch roof supported by small consoles known as modillions. This innovation first occurs in the Regia which was restored in 36 B.C., and is passed over by Vitruvius who probably did not approve of it, being a conservative and a classicist; in fact, nothing contributed more to directing Roman architectural decoration towards the exuberance of the Baroque than the introduction of these modillions.

The frieze reveals the same controlled attraction towards baroque ornament. A scroll of acanthus runs all along the band except on the front which was kept for the inscription. This decorative motif occurs very frequently in Roman art, and there is another fine example, also at Nîmes, from the 'Nymphaeum,' which is a few years earlier than the Maison Carrée. Because of the preference for leaf ornament, it has been possible to classify the various types and use them as the basis of an exact chronology. This comparative study has been conducted by Theodor Kraus and begins with the plaques from the surround of the Ara Pacis.

This is the most impressive monument of Augustan art, both from an aesthetic point of view and from its religious and political significance. It consists of a monumental altar enclosed by a screen of sculptured marble. The upper panels portray scenes from history and mythology while the lower ones, like a tapestry in stone, are carved with huge acanthus plants containing swans sheltering in their symmetrical folds. A comparison of the acanthus of the Ara Pacis with those of earlier monuments reveals its striking exuberance, lively power, and a realism which does not weaken the strictly ordered composition. It seems so alive that some archaeologists have thought it must be an imitation of a real hedge. On the other hand, reliefs dating from the time of Caesar and the Second Triumvirate present scrolls which are elegantly restrained, yet dully geometrical. Kraus has shown that this tendency to austerity coincided with the classic taste of the Neo-Attic

Rome: reconstruction of the Ara Pacis.

school which was much in fashion at Rome in the last years of the Republic. He has also discovered prototypes for the decoration of the Ara Pacis in Pergamene sculptures of the late second century B.C., and it is known that this school freely indulged in a taste for the Baroque which is most brilliantly expressed in the famous frieze of the Battle of the Giants.

Back in Provence, there are examples of these stiff Neo-Attic scrolls on the monument of the Julii at Saint-Rémy built between 30 and 25 B.C. The decoration of the 'Nymphaeum' at Nîmes is already freer and more lively, while the frieze of the Maison Carrée seems to have been executed in the workshops responsible for the Ara Pacis. Although the area set aside for the frieze at Nîmes does not allow the vertical expansion available in the large panels of the Altar, its naturalistic qualities are no less remarkable, and are especially evident on the west side. There are clear stylistic differences between the three sides of the frieze which show that they cannot have been executed by the same sculptor. The artist of the west side has allowed himself to be carried away by the rhythm of his creation to the extent of slightly upsetting the decorative scheme imposed on him.

The Ara Pacis was vowed in 13 B.C.: it was completed and dedicated four years later. The temple at Nîmes inspired by Agrippa must date from before his death in 12 B.C. These dates have rather puzzled art historians: for it is difficult to believe that the Maison Carrée is older than the Ara Pacis which it so significantly resembles. To avoid a detailed, and unsatisfactory argument, it must be admitted that the data resulting from stylistic analysis should probably not be used to arrive at exact chronological conclusions. What is certain is that the Maison Carrée is a typical product of Augustan art, and that its date proves how rapidly the styles in fashion at Rome were reproduced in Provence, which was already highly romanized and had reached the peak of its economic prosperity.

The theater at Arles also dates from this fruitful period, and its architectural and sculptural decoration was selected with one aim in view—the exaltation of the ideals of Augustus. From it comes the famous Venus of the Louvre, a perfect example of the deep understanding of Greek art prevalent during this period, and of the technical ability of contemporary artists. Similar copies formed an integral part of great architectural compositions such as the Maison Carrée.

A final word on the use to which the Maison Carrée was put: it was offered by Agrippa to the colony of Nîmes where the veterans of the Egyptian war had settled, and served as a setting for the ceremonial observances rendered by the town to the Emperor and his associates. In fact, it was not devoted to a funerary cult but to a type of state religion, virtually deprived of a metaphysical side, which was devized by Augustus to serve as a link between the diverse peoples of his Empire. By changing its character, it effectively maintained his hopes for nearly five centuries until the definitive triumph of Christianity.

The Temple of Diana at Nîmes

Another structure at Nîmes will serve as a primary aid to our understanding of the architectural development of Roman religious buildings. The Maison Carrée may be defined as a Roman interpretation of a Greek temple, maintaining the basic principle of the latter: it was made to be seen from the exterior, so that all its important elements may be analysed without any reference to the interior. The so-called Temple of Diana, on the other hand, can only be understood from within.

We must, first of all, note its surroundings. The long, vaulted hall, called the Temple of Diana by the humanists of Nîmes without any real justification, now stands behind the beautiful 'Jardin de la Fontaine' which lies at the foot of Mont Cavalier. This eighteenth-century garden surrounds a spring which was the cradle of the town: for the Gauls personified its beneficial waters as the god Nemausus. When the Roman settlers came into possession, they took over the cult, taking care to give it a setting worthy of their civilization. Thus, from the first century B.C., the sanctuary of Nemausus assumed a civilized appearance contrasting with the rough majesty of the valley where the people of Glanum (Saint-Rémy) continued to worship their eponymous god.

The basic arrangement of the ancient sanctuary can easily be traced in the fountain created by Maréchal in 1739. The water first flowed into an irregular basin which still survives, from which it fed the baths, and finally surrounded a square island, the foundations of which have been restored by copying the antique elements discovered in the course of the excavations. This island was the Nymphaeum, the real sanctuary of the water-god. Its base was surrounded by a sculpured frieze of garlands, the remains of which are preserved in the museum along with the bases of columns enriched with bunches of acanthus like those on the arch of Marcus Aurelius at Tripoli. At each of the four corners twisted columns supported the light roof covering, like that of a summerhouse, sheltering the altar. This was a type of sacred building frequently found in landscapes painted by the Hellenistic schools and their successors, and in the parks and gardens of Roman villas.

It is difficult to estimate the depth of religious feeling still attached to these rustic shrines in the Imperial era. This need not concern us here, but it should be noted that the architect treated the Nymphaeum with a degree of imagination that would never have been permissible in a real temple and which is only rarely found in the decoration of houses and tombs. These minor branches of architecture have often served to try out formulae later put to use in monumental buildings. Thus the canal surrounding the islet of the Nymphaeum widens on the landward side into round or square bays like those decorating fountains in private courtyards. This baroque formula is in perfect harmony with the highly complex ornament of the sacred isle and was still in its infancy at the time of the monuments' construction — in the first years of the reign of Augustus, shortly before the Maison Carrée.

Later on, a group of important buildings arose round the sacred island. These included a large temple of which nothing now remains, apart from the piles forming the foundations and a few decorative features which place it in the late second century A.D. The so-called Temple of Diana was another of these subsidiary additions. It is a rectangular building, the interior consisting of two quite distinct elements: a central hall separated from a surrounding corridor by two walls set on the longer sides. The main, axial entrance gives directly into the hall. Facing it, at the back, is a square aedicule, a stone platform with four columns, cutting the surrounding corridor. The aedicule is flanked by two large doors with straight lintels which lead to small, square chambers cut into the thick back wall. Both the partition walls separating the central hall from the corridor are hollowed into five rectangular niches surmounted by alternate curved and triangular pediments. They extend to human height and are flanked by engaged columns carried on pedestals and supporting an entablature. Two similar niches frame the entrance door. The wall rises a few more courses above the entablature, and then springs into a barrel vault formed of large blocks set parallel to the main axis of the hall and supported by ribs rising above the columns. This magnificent vault was still intact in the sixteenth century, but was partially destroyed in the Religious Wars. Nevertheless, the damaged portions of the structure still held together, bearing witness to its extraordinary solidity. The surrounding corridor is also roofed by a barrel vault composed of large blocks and divided into three sections of varying heights, arranged so that light is admitted at each level.

The building, dated at the turn of the second century A.D., is one of the best examples of the highly original trends in Roman architecture, both as regards its roofing system and its interior decoration. The façade with its great colonnade which has been frequently altered and reworked is imposing enough, but it is clear that the architect concentrated on the interior for his main effects. The overall plan is basilican. Despite its Greek name, this type of building is a Roman creation of the second century. It consists of a huge rectangular hypostyle hall conforming to one of two main types. One has its entrance on one of its shorter sides often with an apse at the far end, the prototype of a Christian church. The other is surrounded by a colonnade and has its entrance in the middle of one of its longer sides. The Temple of Diana belongs to the first group, with a continuous wall replacing the series of arches separating nave from aisles.

Considering the central hall on its own, the building most resembling the Temple of Diana is the striking Doric Nymphaeum on the banks of Lago Albano near Rome which dates from the first half of the first century B.C. There is a whole series of buildings in Italy of the same type. In Cicero's villa at Formiae the center nave communicates with the side aisles and is only separated from them by a Doric colonnade supporting the springs of the three barrel vaults. More often, however, as at Albano and Horace's villa at Tivoli, the building is limited to a central hall with niches hollowed in its walls as at Nîmes. Another example of this type is the auditorium of Maecenas which still survives on the Esquiline and originally belonged to the gardens of Augustus' minister.

Function and Dimensions of Vaulted Halls

This is the right moment to examine some of those vaulted halls which represent the fundamental contribution of Roman architecture to the design of temples and thermae. Vaulted chambers seem to have originally been conceived as imitations of natural grottoes which played an important part in Greco-Roman mythology. They were held to be the dwelling places of supernatural beings, primarily nymphs. These beliefs must have derived from prehistoric cave cults and have been passed on by lands like Crete where they continued to be practised. The gardens of Roman villas very often included artificial grottoes of varying sizes whose religous significance was still fully appreciated. An artificial cavern belonging to a villa of Tiberius has recently been discovered at Sperlonga on the Tyrrhenian coast, on the borders of Latium and Campania. Fish-ponds had been dug in it and a religious and picturesque feature was provided by a sculptured group representing the cave monster, Scylla, devouring the companions of Ulysses.

This derivation makes it clear how the vaulted hall has always been linked with a baroque conception of art. It suggests romantic evocations of the mysterious depths of the earth, the awesome or beneficial beings who inhabit them. It is by no means surprising to learn that it came into fashion at a time of psychological evasion, during the civil wars that brought about the final downfall of the Republic.

The basilicas of this period had no vaulted roofs or apses. Thus it may be doubted whether the westernmost of the three rooms on the front of the Domus Flavia on the Palatine really deserves its recently given title of basilica. Birgitta Tamm thinks that this room was the auditorium or seat of the Imperial Council, but a Danish scholar, H. Finsen, prefers to identify it as a sanctuary. There is also constant discussion as to whether the room was roofed with a barrel vault, or with a timber framework.

To these rooms serving a predominantly religious purpose must be added vaulted halls designed for essentially practical uses, such as those in the thermae—the apodyterium in the Stabian baths at Pompeii for instance—which bear some resemblance to nymphaea, and subterranean galleries like those at Arles. These buildings were roofed with barrel vaults completed by the semi-dome of the apse. These semi-domes were the nearest approach to a cupola in the Augustan period. The oldest examples of cupolas are found in the thermae. Those at Baiae, known as the Temple of Mercury, date from the late, or possibly mid-first century B.C., and include a rotunda 71 feet in diameter—half the area of the Pantheon. This is crowned by a cupola no more than 2 feet thick, its summit pierced by a round light hole; it is constructed of rough tufa. As a rule, the vaulted halls of the Augustan period are of modest dimensions. It may be noted that, in the 'cryptoportici' of Arles, the architect placed two galleries side by side to avoid having too wide a barrel vault.

The earliest example of a groined vault also dates from the Augustan period—that in the House of the 'Cryptoporticus' at Pompeii.

Nero's architects, Severus and Celer, made bold use of the cupola in the east wing of the Domus Aurea. In the middle of this wing was an octagonal hall roofed with a dome. This was an innovation when compared with the usual design for this type of palace as represented in the west wing. A radial plan succeeded a rectilinear one centred on a rectangular courtyard. This octagon was to a large extent open, both to the exterior and to the rooms next to it. The dome was no longer supported by continuous walls, but merely by eight pillars set in an open square. Thus it must have been necessary to distribute the thrusts so as to focus them on these supports. This is the earliest example of such calculations arriving at so bold a solution: a great deal of research must have been needed, but all traces of it have disappeared. The architects of the Domus Aurea also made wide use of rooms with barrel vaults ending in an apse, but these were of modest dimensions.

Domitian's architect, Rabirius, on the other hand, used barrel vaults to cover vast areas, and here we are faced with one of the most controversial problems in the history of Roman architecture, which has been alluded to previously. It concerns the roofing of the two main rooms on the front of the Domus Flavia on the Palatine. In Tognetti's classic reconstruction, the 'basilica' is covered by a terrace supported by a timber roof, while the 'aula regia' is roofed with a barrel vault.

In 1938, Giovannoni formulated the theory that the basilica was vaulted and the aula open to the sky. In 1963, Finsen put forward the opinion that both were roofed with timber. There are, however, good arguments in favor of a vault, especially as one room of the palace of the Flavians retained an even larger barrel vault until recent times. This is the vestibule built by Domitian behind the Temple of Castor, facing the Vicus Tuscus; the adjacent buildings, probably guard-houses, became the Church of S. Maria Antica in the sixth century. The vestibule is a rectangular brick construction measuring 108 feet by 80 feet; it was roofed by a huge semi-cylindrical vault reaching a height of 66 feet above the pavement. The room resembles the aula regia both in its dimensions and in its baroque wall decoration—alternate round and square niches.

There is a direct resemblance between similar vestibules and the central halls of the great Imperial thermae for which the prototype was the Baths of Titus. The only evidence for this building is Palladio's plan which shows a vast hall in the center, the square middle section roofed by a groined vault counterbalanced at the sides by two barrel vaults. Oddly enough, mosaics of the Baths of Trajan at Acholla show an exactly similar arrangement, though the frigidarium in this case must have been unroofed.

Rome: Domus Flavia. Reconstruction by Tognetti showing the vaulted Aula Regia.

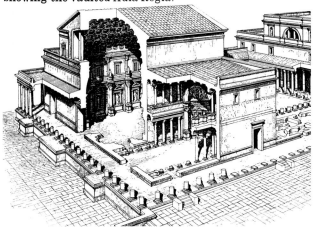

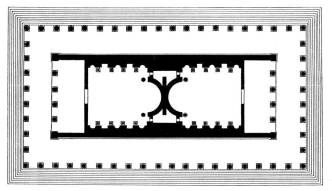

Rome: Temple of Venus and Rome. About 1:1000.

This is the earliest example of the use of a groined vault to cover a large area. The combination of a groined vault and two barrel vaults was very soon, however, replaced by the juxtaposition of three groined vaults which allowed a still larger area to be covered. This combination had already been used in the Baths of Trajan in Rome and was afterwards employed in all the big thermae of symmetrical plan. It is found again in the Basilica of Maxentius above the central nave; in this case it is counterbalanced by two aisles, each roofed by three barrel vaults at right angles to the main axis. The system used in the Baths of Titus—groined vaults counterbalanced by two flanking barrel vaults—occurs in baths on a smaller scale such as the Thermes de Cluny in Paris.

The barrel-vaulted hall with one of its shorter sides closed by an apse and its longer sides ornamented with niches and pseudo-porticoes was used in the second and third centuries for the shrines of some of the larger temples. These included the Hadrianeum, the Temple of Venus and Rome, and Aurelian's Temple of the Sun. A Severan temple recently discovered at Dougga in Tunisia probably also belongs to this type. The Temple of Venus and Rome has often been considered as a Greek type building because of its two symmetrical façades. According to Kähler (whose opinion I do not share) it is really two temples joined together, each possessing a later façade. The interior arrangement of the shrines is essentially Roman.

The Temple of Bacchus at Baalbek

The basilican hall with niched walls could also be incorporated in the plans of many other buildings, especially temples. The most famous and best preserved example is at Baalbek, the Heliopolis of the ancients, in the Lebanon. The Hellenized Syrians of this city worshipped a trinity composed of a god-father, a goddess-mother and a god-son, corresponding to Zeus-Jupiter, Aphrodite-Venus, and Hermes-Mercury. Under the early Empire a vast sanctuary was dedicated to them, which was only completed after several centuries. The chief, immense temple was preceded by a great square courtyard accommodating a monumental altar. A second hexagonal courtyard fronted by a portico formed a vestibule to it. Behind was a second smaller temple ornamented with dionysiac decorations. The exact use of a circular chapel a short distance away is still unknown: its exterior has a remarkable decoration of concave exedrae in the baroque style.

The whole composition owes its effect to its generous proportions and rich baroque ornament. The best preserved building is the small temple known as the Temple of Bacchus, dating from the Antonine period. It is peripteral, with a double row of columns at the 'pronaos' and stands on a lofty platform. At the back of the hall is the 'adyton,' which only the priests were allowed to enter and which forms an independent architectural unit. It stands on a dais and presents, frontally, two wings beneath a double portico. The construction was surmounted by an open pediment and, at the back, was another pediment with columns beneath. The decoration of the 'cella' walls is very similar to that of the Temple of Diana at Nîmes. Tall, engaged columns, standing on pedestals, frame two superimposed series of nitches which originally held statues. The lower ones are surmounted by arches, their archivolts carved with vine branches, the upper ones by pediments. Both are flat against the bare wall which is not hollowed out as at Nîmes, and the columns do not project nearly so much. This lack of depth could be due to structural reasons. The building was probably covered with a barrel vault, and was only lit by the door and a couple of very small windows in the adyton; thus there was insufficient light to stress plastic contrasts. This explanation does

Interior arrangement of the Temple of Venus and Rome. About 1:200.

Baalbek: adyton of the Temple of Bacchus.

not seem wholly convincing, however, as it is obvious that the niches are treated as pure ornaments, embellishments similar to the carvings on the stone doorposts. The architect did not believe in their reality; he did not wish to be led astray or to misdirect others by an illusory space behind the wall. Moreover, recent studies on Roman art show that the attraction for the mysterious and the need to enlarge real with illusory space are first found in Italy, where Etruscan art provides the earliest examples. The appearances of Roman Baroque in Asia are no more than imperfect reflections of the real creative current which was supplied by the West.

It is in Rome, from the first century B.C. onwards, that we find the fore-runners of the decorative feature of niches framed by engaged columns covering the side walls of the Temple of Bacchus at Baalbek. The earliest example occurs in the Temple of Venus Genetrix in Caesar's Forum. This semiperipteral temple on a high platform has a 'cella' with an apsidal end bordered, on each of its longer sides, by seven columns supported on engaged pedestals. There must have been statues in the spaces between the columns, including the famous one of Cleopatra (whose installation caused such a scandal), and the image of the cult was housed in the apse. Caesar's building was destroyed by fire and rebuilt by Trajan, so it is impossible to know if the interior arrangement is part of the original. The interior entablature with a frieze representing cupids celebrating religious rites clearly dates from the early second century. On the other hand, there is no doubt about the Temple of Mars Ultor which was dedicated in 2 B.C. The 'cella' was rectangular, almost square, and widened at the back into a raised apse, destined for the central group of Mars and Venus. On the longer sides were two rows of five columns set on pedestals between the wall pilasters.

The Temple-basilica in Roman Art

The importance of the basilican arrangement of Roman temples must be stressed. It answered the wish to attract to the interior of the 'cella' the traditional ceremonial formerly practised outside. The sacrifice of live animals always took place outdoors on the altar built at the front of the podium, but the advance of religious trends towards syncretism tended to reduce the importance of these sacrifices in favor of direct contact between the worshipper and the god, which took place in the 'cella.' For the revelation of the divine image to achieve its full effect, the idol had to be revealed to the worshipper with the utmost pomp and majesty and, for this reason, was never isolated. Kähler has rightly insisted on the fact that Greek statues are entities offering themselves undivided to the spectator, whereas those of the Romans were almost always integrated in their setting and could only be appreciated along with their background.

In the Temples of Venus Genetrix and Mars Ultor the setting was the apse whose vault evoked both firmament and cave, two concepts which produce a sensation of holiness for most human beings. In the Temple of Diana at Nîmes, as in Syrian temples, the place of honor is given to an aedicule, a kind of pavilion known as 'tetrastyle.' The importance accorded to this construction, the ceiling of which was richly carved with decoration similar to that found in mosaics, shows, in my opinion, that the room was devoted to the worship of a cult, and the fact that the aedicule was added during restoration indicates a wish to accentuate the religious nature of the building. A. Alföldi has shown that this type of building derives from the dais accommodating the throne of an eastern monarch. Thus it confers on the statue the majesty of a conquering king. Later on, the Christians used it, in the shape of the ciborium, to glorify God or to celebrate the triumph of martyrs. The tropaeum built by the Roman Church in the reign of Marcus Aurelius on the site of St. Peter's tomb already took the form of a dais preceding a small apse.

The decoration of the side walls, as we have seen, consisted of a row of columns very close to the wall, or even backing on to it as in the Temple of Diana at Nîmes, with statues in the intervals between. This formula was created by the Greeks and largely borrowed by the Romans who adapted it to serve new ends. The sarcophagus of the Weepers of Sidon dating from the first half of the fourth century B.C. is the earliest preserved example of a portico with columns framing figures. In this case, however, they are not integrated with the architecture: indeed, the artist has consciously made them look as much as possible like live women standing in front of the building, much as actresses in front of stage scenery.

The disappearance of the statues from most ancient buildings prevents us from following the evolution of a Roman type composition though we are able, particularly at Nîmes and Baalbek, to study the development of the niches inserted between the columns as frames for the statues. This is a special application of a combination discovered by the Etrusco-Roman architects of the late second century B.C.

The Tabularium at Rome, dating from 78 B.C., is the earliest example of a monumental composition of arches framed by a series of columns supporting an entablature. Henceforward, this formula was used to obtain varied results, including triumphal arches. At Nîmes and Baalbek, it is employed inside a building in such a way as to form a link with painters of the second and fourth Pompeian styles. Their paintings suggest the existence, above and beyond the wall they decorate, of a world of miracles whose infinite perspectives are visible to us through the supposedly transparent wall. By different means, the architects of Nîmes and Baalbek created a similar illusion. As in the frescoes, the foreground is occupied by a colonnade and the viewer quite naturally expects to find between it and the actual wall a free zone which in fact does not exist. This invitation to attach depth to the composition is further accentuated by the niches which hollow out deep patches of shadow on the wall behind the colonnade. The frames of the niches are treated like those of doors or windows. In the case of funerary monuments, a similar device suggests passage from one world to the next. There is also a carefully contrived alternation of false doors with real ones, which increases the illusion still further.

The Domus Flavia on the Palatine

Domitian (80-96 A.D.) was the first ruler to create a palace really suited to the highly complex role of a Roman Emperor. The same period also saw the construction of the Temple of

Diana at Nîmes, so it is not surprising to find striking similarities between the temple and the Imperial palace. The Domus Flavia was the work of Rabirius, the greatest architect of the age, and consists of two halves in juxtaposition. The east half contains private apartments, while the west wing consists of the ceremonial and state apartments. The center contains a large courtyard, preceded on the north by three reception rooms.

The central room still puzzles architects. Traditionally known as the Aula Regia or Throne Room, the Emperor did in fact hold his audiences there. The vast hall presents the same type of baroque composition as in the plans of the temples at Nîmes and Baalbek. It is built to a rectangular plan and the interior has three niches on each of its shorter sides and five on each of the longer ones. Seven of them are open and form doors. Another, set in the axis facing the main door, housed the throne, and the remainder contained statues. Each projection of the wall framing the niches was fronted by a column of coloured marble. These were crowned by white marble capitals, probably of the composite order and richly executed. Despite its present ruined state, it is easy enough to reconstruct the sumptuous wall decoration of the hall, but the question of its roofing presents architects with a difficult problem. Some believe that it was an open courtyard, but this solution must be discarded for aesthetic reasons, since it would have formed a well weighed down by walls over 66 feet high. Moreover, drainpipes, still visible on the walls, show that the water was carried down the outside. Others have thought that it had a vaulted roof, but the walls do not seem strong enough to bear the thrust. Recently Finsen suggests the hall had a timber framework supporting a four-sided roof. This seems most probable, despite the absence of interior supports—surprising, considering the vast extent of the span. But the most important fact is that the building was roofed. The ceremonies it was designed to house were no longer those of the religion devized by Augustus taking place outside in the sunlight, and for which the Maison Carrée and its surrounding complex were a perfect setting. Here, by candlelight and amid incense, the Emperor received the faithful admitted to his audience.

The principle behind this type of architecture is the total insulation from the natural world of an enclosed space, within which artificial light, gilded stucco, colored marbles, mosaics, the interplay of the curved surfaces of walls and vaults, the rich ornament of capitals and entablatures, solemn music, the glitter of jewels, the gravity of the acolytes—all create a supernatural atmosphere. It will be noted that the development of private houses and buildings designed for public shows and entertainment was directed towards a similar purpose.

The Pantheon

To confirm these conclusions we must consider the Pantheon, a building regarded as typifying the perfection of Roman temple architecture, and luckily today still intact. Its imposing bulk, divided into two distinct sections, stands at the center of Papal Rome, which covers the site of the Campus Martius. The forward part has the appearance of a classical 'pronaos,' with little to distinguish its powerful mass, apart from the fact that its columns are set so as to divide it into three aisles, two of which lead to apses set in the wall and the third to the entrance door. This portico is joined to the body of the building in so clumsy a way that we may well consider it a survival of an earlier construction; and this is supported by the fact that the frieze bears an inscription dedicated to Agrippa, the son-in-law of Augustus, while the bricks of the 'cella' date from 120 to 123 A.D. We now know that the temple was entirely rebuilt by

Hadrian, who decided to leave the inscription to Agrippa. The 'cella' is a vast brick rotunda 142 feet in diameter, crowned by a dome reaching the same height. It is idle to look for precedents for this formula in religious architecture; they are to be found in the thermae, and there is a perfectly sound reason for this apparent paradox.

The colossal bathing establishments of the Imperial era are really enchanted palaces where the power of the sovereign assembled all the marvels of nature for the benefit of his subjects. In the same way, the Pantheon is a microcosm: its dome, the summit of which is open to conduct light into the building, represents the vault of heaven, and all the divinities collected within personify beneficial physical energy. For this reason, just as in the thermae, the splendor of the interior heightened by the use of multi-colored marbles, contrasts with the bare severity of the exterior façades. The spectator is made to feel dizzy when he looks up to the central opening which seems to draw him towards the sky. To prevent the sensation of being crushed by the massive building, the architect devized eight niches in the thickness of the wall of the drum, one of which is occupied by the entrance door: these can be compared with the exedrae of the great courtyard of the temple at Baalbek. At the front of six of these are two columns which seem to support the dome but, in actual fact, it is held by relieving arches which direct the thrusts on to the massive pillars projecting between the exedrae. As in the case of the basilicas, the building has no obvious walls and the spectator's imagination is led on to prolong it to infinity in every direction.

The development of the Roman temple reaches an end in the Pantheon. It is the perfect anti-thesis of a Greek temple in all its elements: interest focused on a completely closed interior, the circular plan, the vaulted roof, structure, materials, and the system of proportion.

Hadrian is deservedly supposed to have been a philhellene and classicist. The break between the Greek spirit of the fifth and fourth centuries B.C. and that of his time appears to have been complete. The Athenians who were his friends and who once elected him archon were as different in their way of life and thought from the contemporaries of Pericles and Socrates as we are from the subjects of Elizabeth I; in fact, the rhetorician, Aelius Aristides, wrote with justification that they had grown into Greek-speaking Romans. When we come to examine Hadrian's villa at Tibur, we shall see how he reinterpreted the heritage of Phidias. The most striking

Rome: Pantheon. Sketch showing construction (after Choisy). About 1:800.

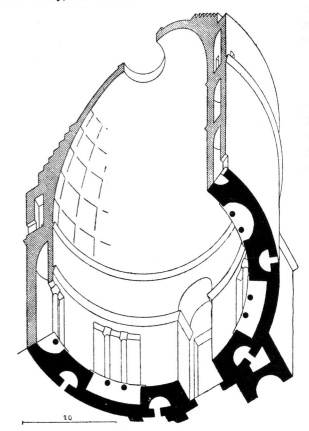

feature of this strange building—whose ruins still make a wonderful impression—is the predominance of curves both in its plan and elevation. In this respect second-century architects once more resemble the great masters of the Baroque—Bernini, Borromini and Le Vau, though the later architects seldom pursued their audacious schemes quite so far.

It would be fascinating to investigate the psychological reasons explaining this overwhelming victory of the curve. Without generalizing, it may be noted that it first appeared in the architecture of theaters and fountains—two types of construction directly linked to the concept of amenity, such an individual feature of Roman civilization, and an elaboration that we shall now trace.

Plates

Pompeii: House of Loreius Tiburtinus

117 The pergola facing the garden with its vine trellis and marble canal.

118 View from the inner rooms towards the garden. All the private apartments were open and faced the garden and its fountains. In the left background is the small marble temple housing the fountain which fed the canals.

119 One of the fountains. An imaginative type of architecture recalling that of a temple or, because of the pebbled background, a natural grotto, haunt of nymphs.

Rome: Baths of Trajan and Golden House of Nero

120 Ruins of the Baths of Trajan, covering the site of the Domus Aurea. The finest surviving example of a Roman brick wall.

121 Detail of the Baths of Trajan.

122 One of the corridors of the Domus Aurea serving the living rooms hollowed out of the Oppian Hill. Walls and vaults are covered with white plaster forming a background for gilded decoration.

123 Structure of the apartments. Note the use of brick lintels, one of the earliest examples of such a feature.

Tivoli (formerly Tibur), Italy: Hadrian's Villa

124 The Canopus. Hadrian had a canal dug in one of the two valleys flanking the spur on which the main buildings of his villa were situated. This canal recalled the Canopus, an arm of the Nile in the neighborhood of Alexandria. Like all the exotic features of the villa, however, this was a highly original and eclectic composition: it made use of contemporary techniques, and was very different from the landscape which served as its basic model.

A large sheet of water led up to a temple of Serapis, a vast vaulted exedra quite unlike any Egyptian building, either Pharaonic or Ptolemaic. At the water's edge were grouped replicas of statues, mainly Greek fifth century models. These classical works were, however, set beneath an airy baroque colonnade.

125 The so-called Teatro Marittimo. This traditional name really refers to a small pavilion completely surrounded by a circular canal. Hadrian is supposed to have retired there alone during the nervous crises from which he suffered at the end of his life.

126 Colonnade of the Teatro Marittimo. This photograph, together with the previous one, shows how new, typically Roman, techniques were used even in circumstances when it would have been possible to revert to classical sources. The entablature of the pavilion offers the usual features of the Ionic order, but is formed of rows of upright bricks. The massive ruins in the background are the remains of the so-called Biblioteca Latina: in fact, they were probably the court apartments.

127 Colonnade and canal of the Teatro Marittimo.

128 A room in the thermae. The right-hand wall has a reticulated surface.

129 The Poikile, a huge rectangular portico enclosing a pool at the entrance to the estate. It has been identified as the Poikile which, according to various texts, Hadrian caused to be built in his villa in imitation of the painted portico of this name at Athens. There is no definite confirmation of this, however.

The Basilica of Maxentius in the Forum Romanum

130 The aisle halls, built of brick, similar to the room in the thermae.

131 Detail of window.

132 General view. The space in the foreground corresponds to the central nave whose groined vaults have collapsed. The springs of the vault can be seen on the wall between the arches. Only one of the aisles has kept its three barrel vaults.

Pantheon, Rome Development of structure of the the dome 1:400, longtitudinal section and plan 1:750.

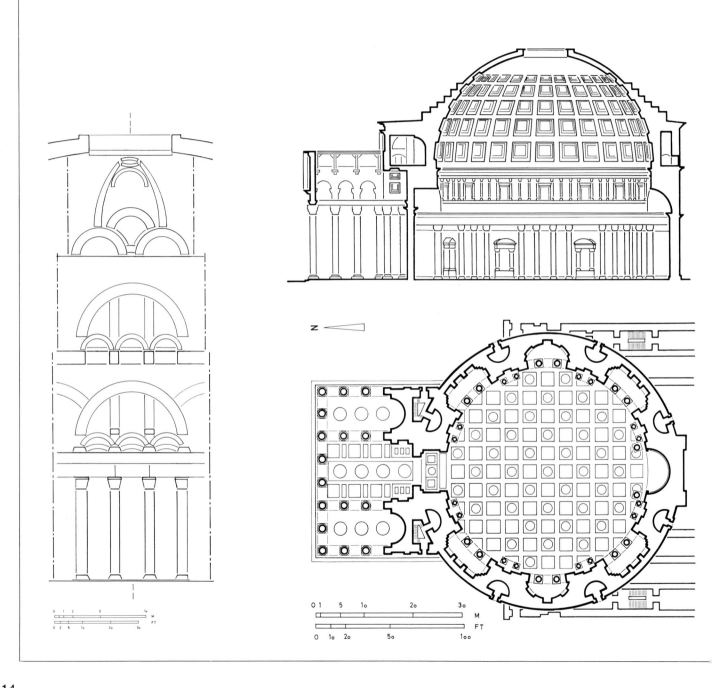

Golden House of Nero, Rome Plan 1:2000,
axonometrical view and plan of octagon hall. 1:500.

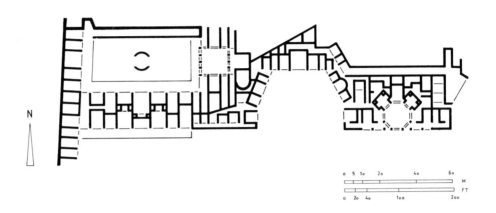

N

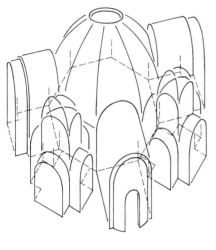

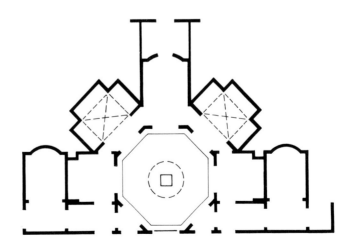

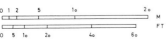

Notes

Severus and Celer, the Architects of Nero

After a brief description of the Domus Aurea, Tacitus gives the names of its creators (Annals, XV, 42). "The master architects and engineers were Severus and Celer who were talented and bold enough to attempt to carry out by technical means what nature refuses, and enjoyed the financial support of the Emperor." In this sentence the inspired historian describes two architects who would otherwise have remained unknown. They were essentially engineers (machinatores) in other words, primarily landscape decorators who succeeded in giving the impression of a vast park in a comparatively small space: the Domus Aurea could not have covered more than 50 hectares.

To create the illusion of infinity was the essential aim of Pompeian painting of the fourth style, and architecture sought the same effects by enlarging rooms with false colonnades against the walls as in the Temple of Diana at Nîmes, or by arranging vistas through a series of rooms where the eye is uninterrupted by walls (as in the Palace of Domitian on the Palatine). The two architects certainly contributed to the diffusion of these theatrical techniques, which must have been especially pleasing to Nero, himself a consummate actor. In the purely technical sphere Tacitus states that Severus and Celer drew up a project for a canal running from Lake Avernus to the mouth of the Tiber, linking Ostia with Puteoli. They very likely also took part in investigations into the balance of stresses and the resistance of materials which prepared the way for the perfection of vaulting techniques, and, in my opinion, were almost certainly the creators of the domed hall of the Domus Aurea, attributed by others to Rabirius. The mechanical devices described by Suetonius, including a revolving dome set in motion by machinery and ceilings which opened to shower the guests with presents, were all within their range. It is doubtful, however, whether they were the authors of the great town-planning scheme for Rome realized after the fire, for the Domus Aurea would probably have occupied all their working time.

Rabirius, the Architect of Domitian

Martial mentions Rabirius in one of his epigrams which praises the architect for his realization of the Flavian Palace on the Palatine. Knowledge of this building is still far from complete as only the north-west half, known as the Domus Flavia, has been fully studied. Here the experts continue to disagree over such basic problems as the roofing of the two main rooms at the front of the building, the Aula Regia and the Basilica which probably should not have this name. The other half, often known as the Domus Augustana, still awaits a full report.

It is difficult to appreciate the originality of Rabirius' work since nothing is known about the layout of the Domus Tiberiana, the other great palace of the Caesars now buried under the Farnese Gardens. The Domus Flavia seems, however, to have been the first really functional Imperial residence and, as such, played a considerable part in the development of royal palaces. Indeed, the palace at Constantinople was directly influenced by it.

The primary aim of Rabirius was to provide an adequate setting for the ceremonies when the Emperor received the homage of his subjects and appeared in full state before foreign delegations. With this in mind he created the Aula Regia, probably taking his inspiration from the atrium where the nobility of ancient Rome used to receive their clients. His chief triumph was the total abolition of interior supports so that there was nothing to impede the view of the Emperor seated on his throne at the back of the hall facing the main door. The walls were articulated by niches containing statues of the gods, so that the Emperor sat among the immortals and on equal terms with them. This feature was borrowed from temple decoration, as we have seen in the cases of the Temple of Diana at Nîmes and the Temple of Bacchus at Baalbek. The vast hall was probably covered with a barrel vault, since Rabirius made the greatest possible use of the opportunities offered by this type of roofing. Another of his buildings in the Forum at the foot of the Palatine, designed as a vestibule to the Domus Tiberiana and occupied by the Church of S. Maria Antica from the sixth century onwards, was certainly roofed with a barrel vault whose dimensions were no less than those of the vault of the Aula Regia. In his design for the apsidal hall adjoining the Aula Regia, Rabirius was probably still influenced by temples of the type of the sanctuary of Venus Genetrix.

Despite recent objections by Finsen, it is likely that this chamber was used for meetings of the Imperial Council. Indeed, there is no other room in the section of the palace open to the public that could have served such a purpose. In this case, the hall was probably a model for the basilicas with apses that were such a feature of the second century, and differed basically from basilicas dating from the Republic and the early Empire.

119

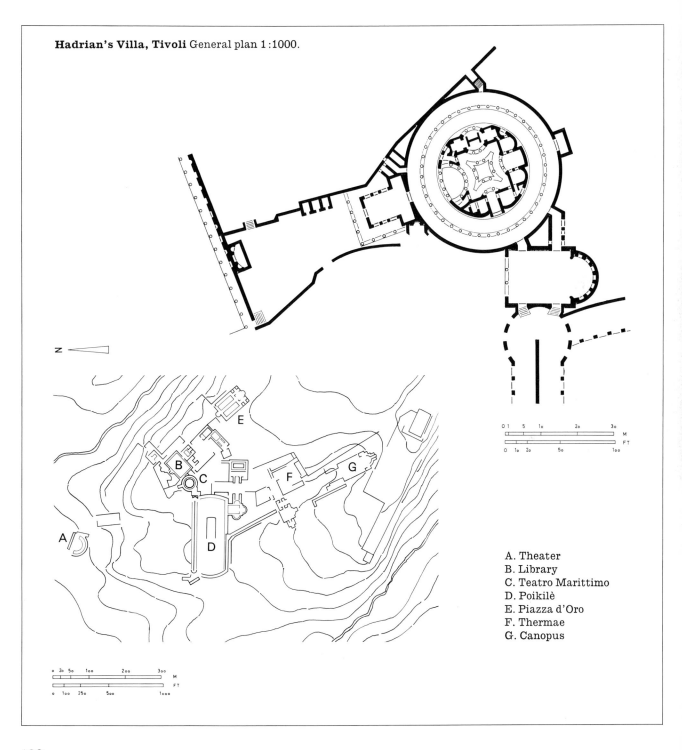

Hadrian's Villa, Tivoli General plan 1:1000.

A. Theater
B. Library
C. Teatro Marittimo
D. Poikilè
E. Piazza d'Oro
F. Thermae
G. Canopus

133

Basilica of Maxentius, Rome Plan and transverse section 1:300, view showing construction.

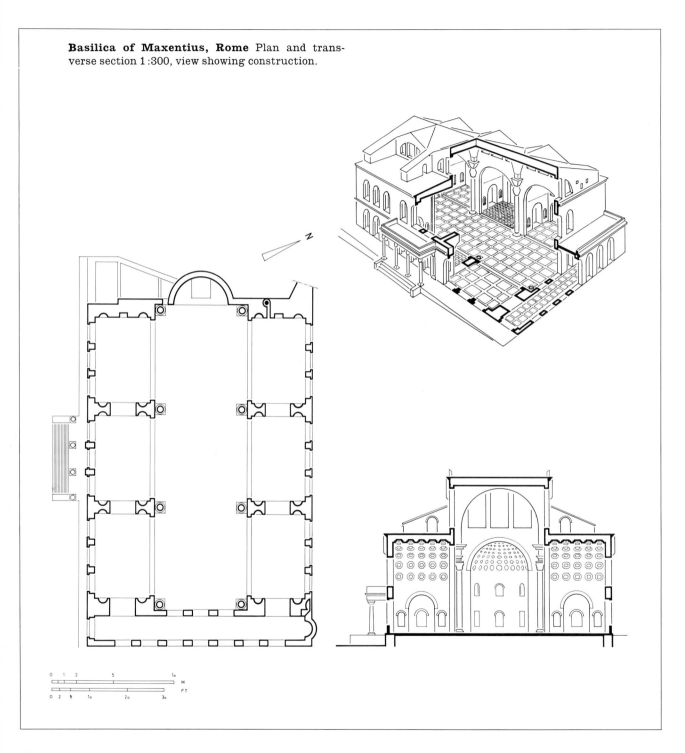

4. Private and Public Amenities

Origins of the Roman House

In the heyday of the Empire, sightseers used to visit a hut made of branches which was preserved on the Palatine. According to their guides, this was where Romulus lived. In fact, the tradition was not so wide of the mark. For, on this famous hill, modern excavations have revealed the foundations of similar huts dating back to the eighth century B.C., so they must have been inhabited by the founders of the Eternal City. Terracotta urns, designed to contain the ashes of the dead, offer miniature reproductions of these huts, thus allowing us to reconstruct them accurately. A century and a half later the houses of Rome began to be more comfortable. The first of them were built by the victorious Etruscans who became masters of Latium under the leadership of Tarquin about 600 B.C. At this time, the king probably lived in the strange Regia on the edge of the Forum at the foot of the Palatine, which later housed the high priests and finally passed to Julius Caesar. The main room of this building was constructed more or less on the principle of a Mycenaean 'megaron,' or great hall, with a central hearth. The real Roman house must have made its appearance during Etruscan domination, but its plan was very different from that of the Regia. The 'atrium' replaced the 'megaron' as the chief room. There is disagreement among experts regarding the early plan of this original and basic component of a Roman house. Some imagine it to have been a courtyard, wide open in the center and bordered by a covered way; the master of the house had his room, known as the 'tablinum,' at the back facing outwards on to a kitchen garden. Others believe that the atrium was completely roofed in, like the central vault of some Etruscan rock tombs which have all the appearance of houses. However this may have been, the Etrusco-Roman house of the fifth and fourth centuries was built to an axial plan. The visitor passed through a vestibule in the middle of the façade into the 'atrium' and thence straight into the 'tablinum' where the master of the house awaited him. The subsidiary rooms were set symmetrically to either side.

Between the fifth and second centuries B.C., the 'atrium' took on its definitive form. It was almost always covered by a roof with a double slope: this had a square opening in the middle above a basin filled with rain water, known as the 'impluvium.' This has sometimes been regarded as a survival of the early courtyard, sometimes as a method of airing and lighting a room which was originally enclosed and thus too dark and unhealthy. In any case, the opening of the 'impluvium' was merely cut out between the criss-cross of the main beams, or bounded by the columns which supported the timber framework. A little later on, the former kitchen garden was surrounded by a colonnade after a fashion which had been current in the Greek world since the fourth century. We now know that this was a purely Italian type, one that was never adopted in the provinces, and seldom found in Rome, even during the early Empire.

The House of Loreius Tiburtinus

One of the most recently excavated houses is in the Strada dell' Abbondanza at Pompeii. Entering by an impressive gateway closed by doors with bronze rings and flanked by seats where visitors would await their patron's pleasure, we find ourselves in the vestibule. This is flanked on the street front by shops which were separate from the rest of the building and rented to tenants. From here we pass into the 'atrium,' from which the bedrooms open out. So far there has been nothing contradicting the usual plan but, after the 'atrium,' we look in vain for the 'tablinum.' Instead, we find ourselves in a small courtyard with a colonnade that gives straight onto a loggia overlooking a large garden. Two rooms with particularly outstanding decorations border the small peristyle. On the left is a dining

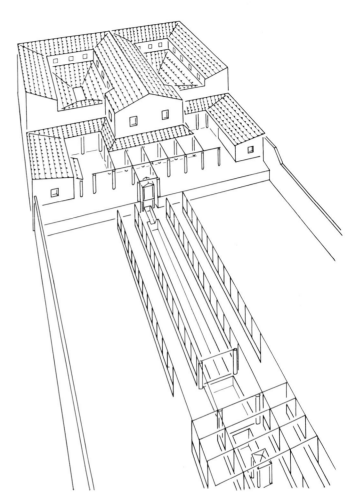

Pompeii: House of Loreius Tiburtinus, reconstruction (after Pane).

room, its walls lined with two rows of frescoes depicting the story of Troy. On the right is a square room with paintings depicting the religious beliefs of the owners, to which we shall return shortly. The long, rectangular garden is divided down the center by a marble canal along which flowed water from a fountain that played beneath the loggia; it contained fruit trees, trellises, arbors full of statues, replicas of famous works of art. Two miniature temples stood at the edge of the canal.

The house is supposed to have belonged either to Loreius Tiburtinus, or to a prominent citizen named Octavius Quartio. However, it enables us to picture the charm of life in Pompeii at the time of the early Empire better than other villas which have been less carefully excavated and restored.

Decoration played an important part, and houses became real museums of painting and sculpture, so that they sometimes looked quite like temples. With the ancients there was only a very slight division between aesthetic and religious feeling.

Pompeian paintings of the second style (second half of the first century B.C.) and of the fourth style (63-79 A.D.) give the illusion that an unreal world is developing behind the seemingly transparent wall. This is especially true of the room at the end of the loggia in the house of Loreius Tiburtinus. Large white panels, in the center of which are medallions portraying the seasons, seem to be hung among airy buildings between which the eye is led towards far distant mysteries.

The Golden House of Nero

The ideals of middle-class life were in no way different from those of the ruling class, but the latter had at their disposal more powerful means for their realization. It was left to Nero, however, to plan the Domus Aurea. Nothing now remains of this palace apart from some dark rooms buried in the ruins of the Baths of Trajan—which were purposely built over it to extinguish the memory of the evil Emperor. These rooms belonged to the main part of the palace backing onto the Oppian Hill. The center was occupied by a trapezoidal courtyard separating two wings. The west wing was arranged round a large rectangular court, while the east wing centred on an octagonal domed hall from which radiated five rooms.

This plan had its inconveniences, for it produced blind corners. The bold mass of the design and the solid construction of the dome, which had light openings in both sides and summit, bear witness to the ability and inventive spirit of its builders, Severus and Celer. The vault rested on ribs transmitting the thrusts to the corresponding angle pillars of the octagon, between which it had been possible to open up the walls so as to communicate with the surrounding rooms. Light came through the hole in the roof. This octagonal hall is sometimes supposed to have formed the remains of the famous banqueting hall described by Suetonius, the dome of which was manipulated by machinery so as to follow the movements of the heavens.

The Domus Aurea did not merely consist of this palace, of which only the ground floor now survives. Nero's grandiose plan had been to link the Imperial Palace built by Tiberius on the Palatine near the modest House of Augustus, with the gardens of the Esquiline that had been left to the Caesars by Maecenas. This meant surrounding the whole of the east side of the valley of the Forum, starting from the House of the Vestals, with buildings. There are remains of the first attempt, known as the Domus Transitoria—which indicates its function as a link—decorated with graceful paintings. The plan, however, could not be fully realized until after the great fire of 63 A.D. which swept away the squalid, populous quarters of that area.

Nero turned this space into a park with a lake in the middle, on the future site of the amphitheater. The enterprise was rated a piece of monstrous folly but Nero was a good town-planner; and the regulations he drew up for the reconstruction of other districts destroyed by the fire were highly intelligent both from the artistic and the practical point of view. His idea of setting up a green belt in the middle of the fearful tangle of houses forming the city center was sensible. The total area of the park was smaller than that of the Farnese Gardens on the site of the Palatine. The idea of a triumphal avenue bordered by a colonnade linking the park with the Forum could now be fulfilled, and the old square thus acquired towards the east a pleasing architectural perspective. The chief fault of the Domus Aurea was that it was a country house in town. The practical Romans disapproved of wasting land whose value was high (a feeling which still exists today). In the country, however, no objection was made to great landowners, such as Hadrian, surpassing Nero's most lavish projects.

Hadrian's Villa at Tibur (Tivoli)

The entire group of buildings covers about 380 acres on the steep slopes of the Apennine

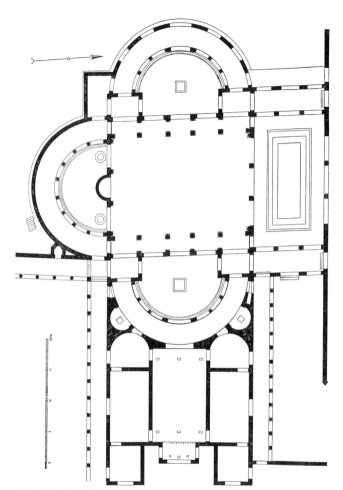

Hadrian's Villa: plan of the large dining hall (after Kähler). About 1:500.

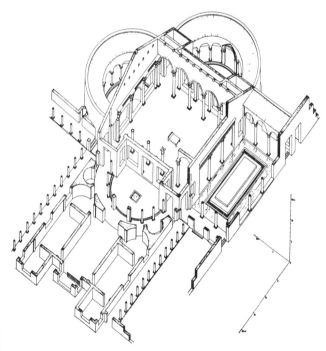

Tivoli: Hadrian's Villa. Axonometric reconstruction of the great dining hall (after Kähler).

foot-hills. The visitor first enters an oblong space surrounded by walls and a colonnade 760 feet by 318 feet, in the center of which was a large pool. This is traditionally known as the Poikilè after the famous 'stoa' at Athens which, according to some reports, Hadrian had copied in his villa.

The first group of buildings is set to the east above the so-called Poikilè. First we cross an attractive rotunda fringed by a canal forming a small island in the center, with a villa built on it. After this comes a rectangular courtyard with colonnades leading, on the north side, to two complex buildings that have been called libraries, but that were more probably luxurious banqueting halls. On the east side are two sets of rooms paved with pretty black-and-white mosaics decorated with delicate scroll ornaments typical of contemporary taste. These were probably guest-rooms, and are set on either side of a wide corridor leading to a chapel. Another group, arranged round a vast peristyle, overlooks the one just described from the east. This has been identified as the remains of an earlier villa begun under the Republic and later transformed into the main Imperial residence. Further up the hill in the same direction we reach the most lavish part of the whole layout. This consists of a huge square courtyard with colonnades, originally surrounded by gardens, preceded by a vestibule in the shape of a curvilinear octagon, roofed by a dome.

Another pavilion, recently restored, due to the generosity of a large industrial company, faces the vestibule, and here the plan assumes the form of a curvilinear square with concave sides. A dome rested on the serpentine entablature, the weight of which was solely supported by pillars and columns. Kähler has shown that this airy pavilion, flooded with light from the wall openings, and apparently defying the laws of gravity, derived from the domed hall of the Domus Aurea.

Further down the hill, compact blocks of red brick contrast with these buildings. This complex prolongs one of the sides of the Poikilè and contains fountains and 'nymphaea' together with vast vaulted halls, one of which is shaped like a clover leaf. To the south, these buildings join on to a group of baths forming part of yet another huge complex branching off at an angle from the center of the side of the Poikilè. Here is a valley running along the foot of the mountain and, in its southern half, was dug a vast oblong canal, 390 feet long, a gigantic replica of the Euripus which enlivened the garden of Loreius Tiburtinus and, similarly, bordered by statues. At the far end of the canal stood an enormous vaulted apse resembling a grotto which was dedicated to Serapis, the husband of Isis and the chief god of Hellenistic Egypt.

Hadrian called this valley Canopus, after a suburb of Alexandria where an arm of the Nile led to a temple of Serapis. At one point on the bank was the statue of an old man symbolizing the Nile and, further on, a sufficiently scaly crocodile; the other statues in the vicinity— copies are now in the museum—reproduce the

Hadrian's Villa: axonometric reconstruction of the hall of the small palace (after Kähler).

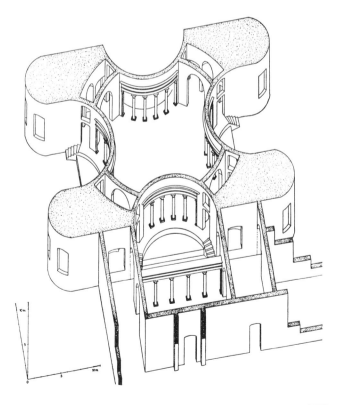

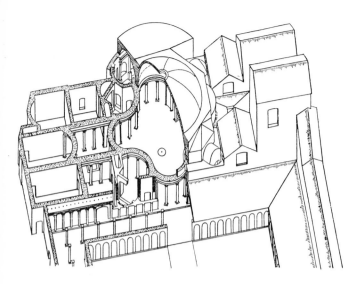

Hadrian's Villa: reconstruction of the domed hall of the Piazza d'Oro (after Kähler).

best known creations of classical Greece. They represent Hadrian's well-known love of classicism, and we must now examine the setting of these masterpieces. A graceful Corinthian colonnade binds the curve of the Euripus to the answering one of the Serapeum. Its entablature is alternately straight and arched to frame the statues; it is impossible to imagine a less classical form of composition or one so far removed from a possible design by Ictinus. To Hadrian and his contemporaries, Greek statues or pictures, whether originals or exact copies, were delightful objects whose fine points had to be brought out by placing them in a contrasting setting. The classicism of this period was quite different from that of the Augustan age, which really recreated a classical style. It was more of an eclectic dilettantism comparable with that of eighteenth century France.

In the vestibule of the Piazza d'Oro and in the Serapeum are examples of the umbrella vault composed of a series of triangular, spherical sections, giving the impression of veils inflated by the wind. The type of vault, set on an alternately concave and convex entablature, as in the Piazza d'Oro, recurs in another building, known as the Accademia, behind the Serapeum.

Despite the vast scale of its peristyles and baths, Hadrian's villa is predominantly a large park dotted with buildings, none of which completely dominates the others. Though the original vegetation has disappeared, it has fortunately been replaced by fine trees, so that we can capture some idea of the perfection attained by the Romans in the art of garden design.

The Public Amenities of the Thermae (Baths)

We know that even though Hadrian's palaces contained so many luxurious baths, he did not spurn the use of the public thermae. These institutions had the same attraction for the Romans as our present-day clubs. Many citizens probably had no other choice: those who lived in large apartment blocks, after the pattern of the Horrea Epagathiana at Ostia, had no running water in their apartments, and neither did most private houses—apart from fountains in the

Hadrian's Villa: plan of the domed hall of the Piazza d'Oro (after Kähler). About 1:700.

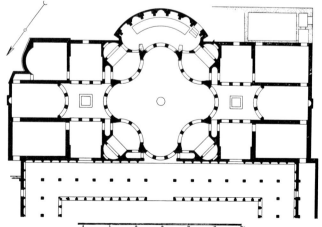

middle of their courtyards. Thus the buildings of the thermae played an essential part in the life of Roman cities. Even the smaller towns possessed several baths, and they were also built for the use of mine-workers who, as a class, were otherwise badly treated. The largest and most luxurious examples were, of course, in Rome.

The Baths of Diocletian

The building forms an almost perfect rectangle, 411 yards by 393 yards, covering over 32 acres. The 'calidarium,' or hot-room, formed a great projection in the center of one of the longer sides, while the individual rooms of the vast building were perfectly symmetrical in relation to the axis passing through the center of these sides. The essential installations were all arranged round this axis. From north-east to south-west there were, successively, a cold pool open to the sky, 2,734 square yards in area, and a great hall known as the 'cella media,' roofed with a barrel vault; off this led several smaller cold pools. This hall and the vast rotunda of the tepidarium which succeeded it were turned into the Church of Santa Maria degli Angeli by Michelangelo, and the Church largely maintains the arrangement and even the decoration of the ancient building. The exedra which now forms the entrance of the Church belonged to the 'calidarium' which was rectangular, and originally contained three altar apses set to form a cross with the surviving one.

On either side of the center block were two symmetrical wings. Two vestibules flanked the large cold pool and led to dressing-rooms closed by apses at each end. After the bathers had undressed they could either plunge straight into the cold pool or go into one of the 'palaestra,' great rectangular courts with colonnades, set behind each end of the 'cella media.' These contained all the equipment required for games. After the bathers had warmed themselves up

Great Hall of the Baths of Diocletian: sectional view. About 1:1250.

here, they could either go back to the 'frigidarium' and plunge into one of the pools bordering the 'cella media' or go straight to the 'calidarium' through a series of heated rooms that completed the south-west side of the building. The vast complex stood in a park enclosed by a retaining wall, the outer side of which presented a series of alternate square and rounded exedrae. The largest of these exedrae was set in the axis of the 'calidarium' and gives its shape and name to the square into which the Via Nazionale now runs.

The Plan of the great Imperial Thermae

The building of these baths was initiated by Maximilian after his African victory of 297, but they were not completed until 305. The architect limited himself to applying on a grand scale and with a few changes of detail a plan which had been put into practice two hundred years earlier in the Baths of Trajan. The scheme was again reproduced at Rome, notably in the Baths of Caracalla, and spread rapidly throughout Italy and the provinces. The earliest baths, on the other hand, like those at Pompeii, were much more simple; they contained no pools large enough for swimming. Thus, the development of thermal architecture offers special proof of the influence exercised on provincial builders by the master architects of the capital. The projects which they completed served as models throughout the Empire. Doubtless less complex baths were built in the second and third centuries, lacking the symmetrical plan typical of the great Imperial thermae, but here too, the precedent came from Italy, its most notable application being found in the thermae of Hadrian's Villa. Nevertheless there were regional variations. In hot countries, for instance, hot rooms were considered of less importance, but there was an increase in the number of cold rooms for use during the siesta period; naturally, the reverse applied in cold climates. Here and there

Rome: plan of the Baths of Diocletian. About 1:2500.

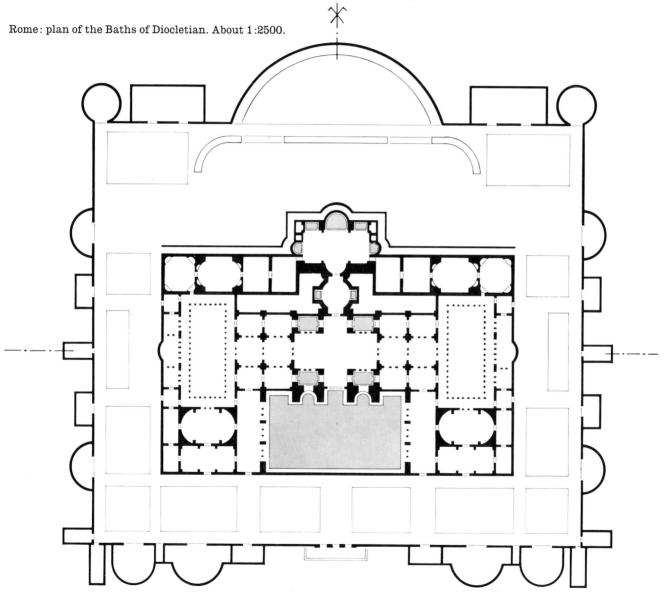

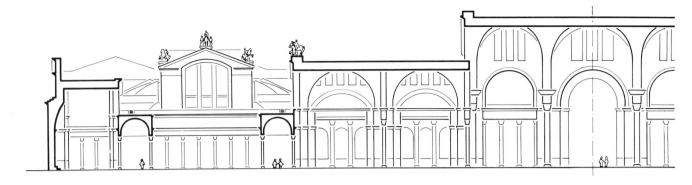

Baths of Diocletian: sectional view.

may be found isolated attempts by original architects, but even so, almost every city prided itself on having baths exactly similar to those of the capital.

Such diffusion made a large contribution to the development of the most original tendencies of the dynamic architecture of the Romans. The risk of fire compelled them to do away with timber roofs and provide all the halls with vaults. Thus, the great Imperial thermae only appeared from the time when the general employment of groined vaults allowed the roofing of almost boundless areas. These juxtaposed groined vaults were particularly used in the 'cellae mediae' of the 'frigidarium,' vast waiting-rooms preceding the cold water pools. Their weight was upheld either by massive pillars or, as in the Baths of Antoninus at Carthage, by colossal granite columns. The hot-rooms were more often covered by domes and, for this reason, built to a circular or polygonal plan, as in the Baths of Caracalla. The Baths of Diocletian, with their rectangular 'calidarium,' are an exception to the rule. At Tibur, Hadrian's architect clearly could not curb his imagination, especially in the small baths, where an octagonal hall with four convex sides was roofed with an extraordinary undulating dome. As a rule, however, the thermae were solidly built, and the

cement used in them was more resistant than in any other building. Thus large blocks of rubble from thermae on Roman sites that have been almost obliterated are often the only signs of ancient civilization.

The astonishing resistance of the Thermes de Cluny, the superstructure of which still survives after eighteen centuries in the heart of Paris, shows that Gallo-Roman architects were by no means behind their colleagues in this respect. Their assessment of the resistance of materials was extremely accurate and, in the upper portions, they made use of soft stones, such as pumice, for preference. In Africa, where scarcely any heavy form of ceramic was manufactured, it is strange to find rough-stone cut exactly to the size of bricks in those parts of buildings where bricks were normally used.

One of the architects' chief concerns was avoiding loss of heat from the interior—one more reason for their preference for vaults, and for making walls as thick as possible. This also led to doing away with windows—which also prevented anyone from looking in when the establishments were open to women (mixed bathing was permitted in some periods, but was forbidden by Hadrian). Thus the outer façades presented vast areas of bare surface beneath the

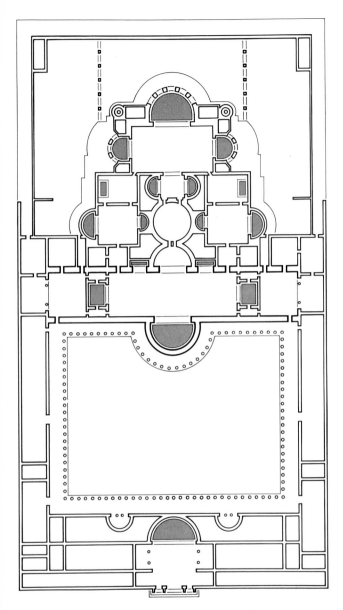

Trier: plan of the Imperial Thermae. About 1:2000.

ing to contrast the austerity of the wall of the thermae with the rich decoration of the wall surrounding the park. Above all, they wished to establish a complete antithesis between the severe, purely functional façades and the riotous baroque decoration of the interior.

The Decoration of the Thermae: A Triumph of Baroque

Baths, together with theaters, were the chosen domains of Roman baroque ornament. In the Baths of Diocletian, the great open-air pool, a real lake of marble, reflected a monumental façade with five great niches alternately curved and rectangular in accordance with the pattern of a theater stage. Within them were ranged on three levels marble aedicules sheltering statues. The interiors were just as ostentatious, as we can see from Santa Maria degli Angeli which has retained some of the original decoration. Contrasting forms and colors were to be found everywhere. The former resulted from the interplay of the curved and straight borders of pools and fountains, the latter from the use of rare and costly materials. There was marble of every hue, and also granite and porphyry, which were employed both for columns and for the basins of fountains and small baths. The basin carved from a single block of porphyry 47 feet in circumference, now standing in the center of the great rotunda of the Vatican Museum, came from the Baths of Diocletian, and the two fountains in the Piazza Farnese are each made from a small bath from the Thermae of Caracalla. Capitals and entablatures were elaborately carved and figured capitals are particularly outstanding.

Those from the Thermae of Caracalla represent Hercules, the Emperor's patron, and an extraordinary capital from the Baths of Antoninus at Carthage shows on each face a veiled old man, probably Saturn, his legs replaced by

wavy outlines of domes and vaults, unbroken by a single window. The architects could have concealed this bareness by surrounding the building with colonnades, but they did not do so, preferr-

Rome: plan of Baths of Caracalla. About 1:2700.

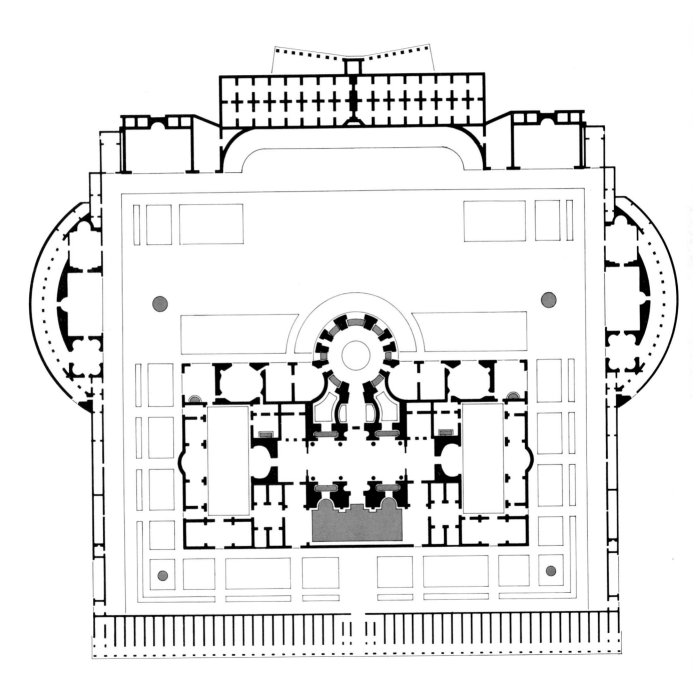

dragons which are controlled by winged genii.

The vaults were faced with gold or brilliant glazed mosaics. The Romans began to make use of this technique for the decoration of baths and fountains from the first century A.D. onwards. Later it was revived for the ornamentation of Christian churches, reaching its culminating point in the Byzantine period.

A form of rapture, induced by Byzantine mosaics, was not a Christian innovation. It was a legacy from Roman art which first attempted to achieve it in private houses by the paintings of the second and fourth Pompeian styles. Mosaic, 'musivum opus' was kept solely for the facings of walls and vaults. Floors were formed of tessellated pavement which, from the early second century, had black figures standing out against a white background in Italy, or a polychrome background in Africa and the East.

The decorations at the Ostia thermae usually represented the most sensual or moving subjects in Greek art. The famous Laocoon group now in the Vatican was discovered in the ruins of the Baths of Trajan, and the magnificent nude figure of Aphrodite in the Museo Nazionale Romano was taken from the thermae at Cyrene in 1913. Like the temples, the baths served as museums and cultural centers, since they also contained libraries.

Political Significance of the Thermae

The government which spent vast sums on the construction of these buildings and provided them with a liberal supply of water brought at great expense by the aqueducts, knew that this expenditure was not in vain. For it contributed to the psychological reaction indispensable to a regime which, like modern totalitarian states, could not afford to lose the support of public opinion despite centralization of power.

Trophies and monuments were often found in the thermae; they served to remind visitors that their enjoyment was procured and guaranteed by the power and might of the Emperors. The thermae were the most effective instruments of the Emperors' social policy: the poorest members of the community—including slaves— enjoyed here the same luxuries as the highest nobility.

For this reason, the baths' architectural principles were applied to other similarly destined buildings. We have already seen that the Pantheon, the most typical of the Imperial temples, offers the same architectural characteristics as the thermae; and some archaeologists have wrongly been led to suppose that the huge rotunda originally formed part of the nearby Baths of Agrippa.

The Influence of Thermal Architecture: The Basilica of Maxentius

A building contemporary with the Baths of Diocletian, the Basilica of Maxentius, shows even more clearly how the plans devized for the thermae were transposed to suit other schemes whose purpose was also to bring popular assemblies into contact with the ruling class. The enormous brick vaults of the Basilica of Maxentius, or Constantine, dominate the Via Sacra near its junction with the Forum, between the Temple of Venus and Rome and a rotunda, now forming part of the Church of SS. Cosma e Damiano. This section of the Velia, as the district was known in antiquity, was entirely reconstructed between 306 and 312 by Maxentius, the son of Maximinian. The building dates from the early fourth century. The temple of Venus and Rome built by Hadrian, was restored during the same period, and the Basilica was near completion when Constantine entered Rome.

We have already discussed the origins of the basilica, a Roman creation known by a Greek name. The Basilica of Maxentius, however, had scarcely anything in common with its predecessors, particularly the Basilica Aemilia and the Basilica Julia which bordered the Forum Romanum, apart from the use to which it was put and its long rectangular plan. Instead of a central nave surrounded by a forest of columns or arches, as in the Basilica Julia, its interior consisted of a single space, the largest hall of ancient times, 263 by 167 feet and divided, despite its vast area, by only four pillars which supported the vaults. The central nave, 263 by 82 feet, was covered by three groined vaults, and each of the two flanking sections by three barrel vaults set at right angles to the axis. Only the roof of the north collateral now survives, because it was built against the hill of the Velia which had been hollowed out to support it. The original plan of Maxentius included a single apse at the west end opposite the entrance. Constantine, however, decided to change the orientation of the building, constructing a new apse in the middle of the long north side and placing opposite it, on the south side, a door giving on to the Via Sacra. The western apse contained a colossal statue of the Emperor, and the northern apse housed the raised tribunal.

Architects unanimously stress the similarity of this building to the large 'cellae' of the thermae. It also foreshadows the vaulted cathedrals of the Middle Ages. The reign of Constantine saw the building in Rome of the first monumental Christian basilicas: St. Peter's, the Lateran, S. Paolo fuori le Mura, and S. Lorenzo. These all had timber roofs, and Western churches followed their examples and kept to this type of covering. Vaulted churches reigned supreme in the East, however, especially at Constantinople. Churches like S. Sophia with its domes and its bold, austere façades contrasting with the decorated interior are aesthetically in direct succession to the Roman thermae. Similar effects were again used in Renaissance Italy. With the Church of S. Maria degli Angeli and the Parthenon as models and intermediaries, it is possible for Bramante's and Michelangelo's St. Peter to help us recreate the atmosphere of the Baths of Caracalla and Diocletian.

Buildings Designed for Public Entertainments

Quite often the government offered Roman citizens amusements which both stopped them from thinking about the political situation, and established and strengthened a bond between the Emperor and his subjects, similar to that sought by modern dictatorships. Every city throughout the Empire, no matter how small, had at least one theater, circus, or amphitheater. The majority as a rule had at least two of these three types of building. In countries such as Gaul, where cities were few and far between, theaters were built in the open country near old native sanctuaries where the peasant population used to gather. Two such theaters associated with a country temple may be seen in the immediate vicinity of Paris: at Genainville in the Vexin and Champlieu in the Oise.

We should note that this wide diffusion of buildings destined for public entertainment, together with the spread of thermae, contributed to directing Roman taste in architecture to baroque solutions. Examples are two monuments in Tripolitania, both remarkably well restored: the theaters at Leptis Magna and Sabratha.

The Theater at Leptis Magna

The theater at Leptis was built at the beginning of the Empire. Three inscriptions have been discovered in which an influential resident of the Punic town—which was still only slightly romanized—dedicates the building, which he had had constructed at his own expense, to the Emperor Augustus in the years 1-2 A.D. He was Annobal (or Hannibal) Rufus, a member of the Tapapi, a famous Phoenician family. The inscription is carved both in Latin and Phoenician which shows better than anything the desire for integration which was the aim of this magnificence.

In a previous chapter, we made a rapid survey of the problem set by the construction of the 'cavea,' the stepped semi-circle, of a theater. The site of Leptis, a coastal plain divided by a river mouth, is completely flat. Therefore, Annobal's architect had the substructure of the lower tiers hewn from the rock. The excavated rubble was thrown outwards and held in position by a casing of masonry so as to form supports for the middle rows. Only the top tiers rest on massive stone and cement pillars. From outside, the semi-circular section of the theater appears as a vast, compact drum only pierced by five vaulted passages leading to the 'praecinctio' the promenade dividing the tiers half-way up the 'cavea.' The 'introvert' character of the building —which has rightly been compared with that of a mausoleum—agrees with one of the dominating tendencies of Roman architecture. This is more accentuated at Leptis than in the wholly Roman theaters and amphitheaters, with their arches, whose connections with strictly functional considerations have already been stressed. At each end of the 'cavea,' however, the architect set vaulted rooms which were used as shops, a rare individual touch, probably justified because the chief market was close by. Another remarkable feature was to be found behind the stage. Instead of a massive, high wall like the one at Orange, the architect designed a large square with a colonnade forming a sanctuary of the Imperial cult.

A temple dedicated to the posthumously deified Emperors was set up in the center, a reminder of the joint religious and political character of the foundation. Annobal Rufus and his descendants also hit upon a highly ingenious method of blending their traditional form of worship with that of the new ideology. A platform was set apart in the center of the promenade at the top of the 'cavea' on which was erected a temple dedicated to Ceres, the Demeter of the Sicilian Greeks, who had been adopted four centuries previously and had become one of the chief protectresses of Africa. This idea was directly inspired by Pompey who had set up a temple of Venus in the same position in his theater in Rome. The temple at Leptis was not consecrated until the reign of Tiberius, but appears to have been included in the original plans.

We must now turn our attention to the stage —the essential part of any theater. In this case it was a platform raised three feet above the level of the orchestra which it dominated by a straight wall indented with niches. It had a wooden floor which has, of course, disappeared; only the retaining walls are left. It has, however, been possible partially to reconstruct the imposing decorative feature which closed it to the rear. This is formed of four massive blocks of masonry with three great apses set between them; at the back of these were doors which connected the stage with the corridors behind. The columns and entablature imitating a palace front, originally set up in the second century, have been re-erected against the massive bulk of the 'frons scaena.'

The Theater at Sabratha and the God of the Frons Scaena

To realize how grand an effect could be produced by this form of decoration, we must turn to Sabratha, the westernmost of the three

Phoenician cities of Tripolitania. The theater, built at the start of the third century, was one of the ostentatious gifts made by Septimius Severus to his family's native country. In this case, it has a built-up façade which may be compared with the curved exterior, with its double row of arches, of the exactly contemporary amphitheater at El Djem. It is interesting to see how the architect of the theater, though using exactly the same design as that of the amphitheater, has managed to soften the overall effect. His arches are treated as the bays of a triumphal arch with moulded archivolts supported by pilasters, and the order framing them again consists of pilasters instead of the more usual engaged columns. In this way the fierce contrasts of light and shade are weakened without loss of vigor to the structure as a whole.

The play of light would be enough to bring the ruin back to life, but sculpture, too, has a part in reminding us of the actors. At Sabratha the statues have disappeared, but those at Leptis have been rediscovered, and show gods mingling with mortals. At Sabratha, the 'pulpitum' which offers the usual rhythm of alternate round and square niches has an almost unique form of relief decoration. It consists of scenes from mimes and tragedies. Contrary to what has frequently been said, the theater still survived in the third century and repertory pieces were still performed.

We must stress the very widespread influence of the device of the 'frons scaena' on other types of building. There have already been examples of its use in domestic, palatial and religious architecture. Domitian's Aula Regia on the Palatine, the interior decoration of the Temple of Diana at Nîmes and of the Temple of Bacchus at Baalbek, and the grandoise façade dominating the main pool of the Baths of Diocletian are all related to it. Above all, theater stages offer a remarkable connection with monumental fountains and 'nymphaea' which reproduce the same device of alternate round and square niches, as we have seen in the sanctuary of Nemausus. Similarly, fountains often used to play in the niches of the stage 'pulpita.' Sometimes, especially from the third century onwards, the whole orchestra space was transformed into a pool in which scantily dressed female dancers performed aquatic ballets.

Significance of the Baroque Style

The search for comfort led Roman architects to solutions very close to those they had discovered in their attempts to express the religious feelings of their society. The amenities they enjoyed appeared to the citizens of the Empire as the natural result of Rome's power.

Because of their sense of justice and piety, the Roman people and their Emperors were granted by providence the mission of bringing order and happiness to the universe. While this is not the place for a detailed examination of such an ideology, we must note that it expressed itself in forms that seem to be contradictory but are in fact complementary and capable of realization by the same technical means. There are the immovable, austere masses of functional architecture representing the might of the Empire and, also the style that may well be termed Baroque. By its preference for curved outlines and rich ornamentation, Roman Baroque expressed the ideas of fertility, abundance, freedom, happiness and communion with the vital forces of nature. It was perfectly suited to functional architecture, and thus every Roman building appears as a miniature of the Empire where the strength of the legions spun out along the 'limes' allowed the Mediterranean peoples to enjoy the only period of peace they have known throughout their history.

Plates

Leptis Magna (Tripolitania): The Theater

155 Sanctuary of the Imperial cult, formed of a temple surrounded by a colonnade. This was built behind the stage in accordance with customary usage.

156 The semi-circular cavea with its tiers of seats.

157 Detail of the cavea, showing the staircase giving access to the tiers of seats. Further up was the praecinctio, the open gallery separating the blocks of seats, or maeniana.

158 Decoration on the parapet of one of the official boxes, with a few letters of the inscription. This is dedicated to Caninius, proconsul of Africa in the early years of the Christian era.

Sabratha (Tripolitania): The Theater

159 Outer façade of the cavea. The arch openings are dwarfed by the masonry as in the contemporary amphitheater at El Djem (plates 69-70). The usual engaged columns are here replaced by pilasters.

160 The restored stage. In the foreground, the actual stage and sculptured pulpitum. The background consists of the superimposed columns of the frons scaena which imitates a palace façade and frames the entrance and exit doors used by the actors. This type of composition, with its projections and recessions, and its alternate curves and straight lines, had a decisive influence on the origins of baroque architecture.

161 The central or royal door with the middle niche of the pulpitum below. The bas-relief shows Septimius Severus offering sacrifices to the gods of Africa.

162 General view of the pulpitum whose rhythm echoes that of the frons scaenae. The sculptures of the flanking niches recall the plays given in the theater.

Palmyra: Temple of Bel

163 The central cella, surrounded by a colonnade with Corinthian columns. The original bronze capitals were pillaged by the natives.

164a Detail of a pilaster ornamented with deeply incised palmettes and scrolls.

164b Detail of an Ionic capital surmounting one of the engaged columns of the exterior wall of the sanctuary.

165 Exterior side wall of the sanctuary. Its rhythm is created by pilasters with Corinthian capitals. The holes scattered over the regular surface were the work of thieves who stole the bronze tenons fixed in the wall.

166 One of the thalamoi. These chambers are at the two ends of the cella: they formed the private apartments of the god and housed the statues of his cult. They are the equivalent of the adyton at Baalbek (plate 88.)

167 Detail of the ceiling of one of the thalamoi. It consists of large slabs carved in high relief.

Palmyra: Funerary Towers

168 General view of the necropolis. This Valley of the Dead is situated outside the oasis of Palmyra and is surrounded by the desert on all sides.

169 Façade of the Tower of Elahbêl. The sarcophagus of the builder may be seen at second floor level in the only window opening of the front.

170 Interior of the tower. Each of the superimposed chambers within the monument contains a series of niches or columbaria. These were originally closed by stelae carved with the effigies of the dead, but they are now to be found in most museum collections throughout the world.

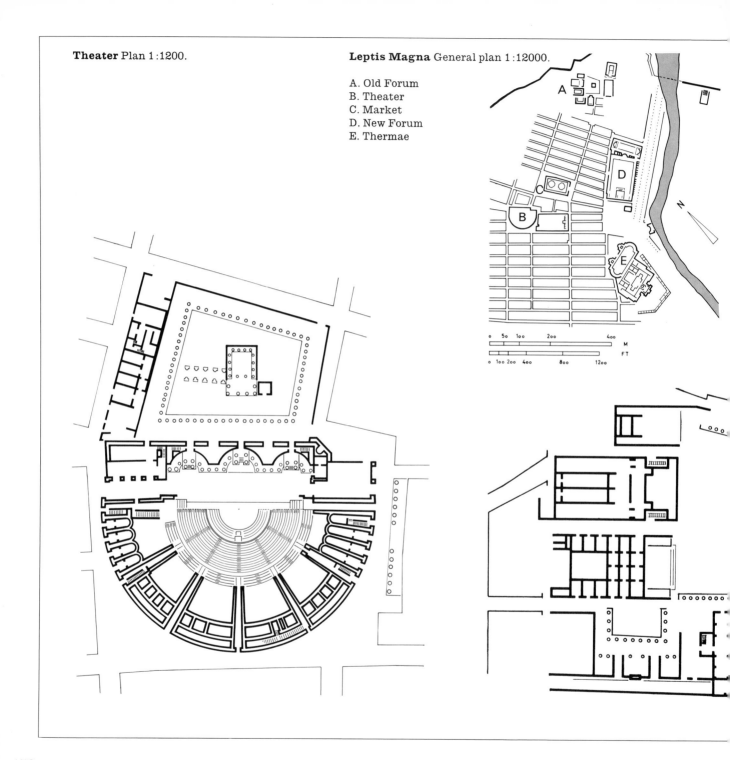

Theater Plan 1:1200.

Leptis Magna General plan 1:12000.

A. Old Forum
B. Theater
C. Market
D. New Forum
E. Thermae

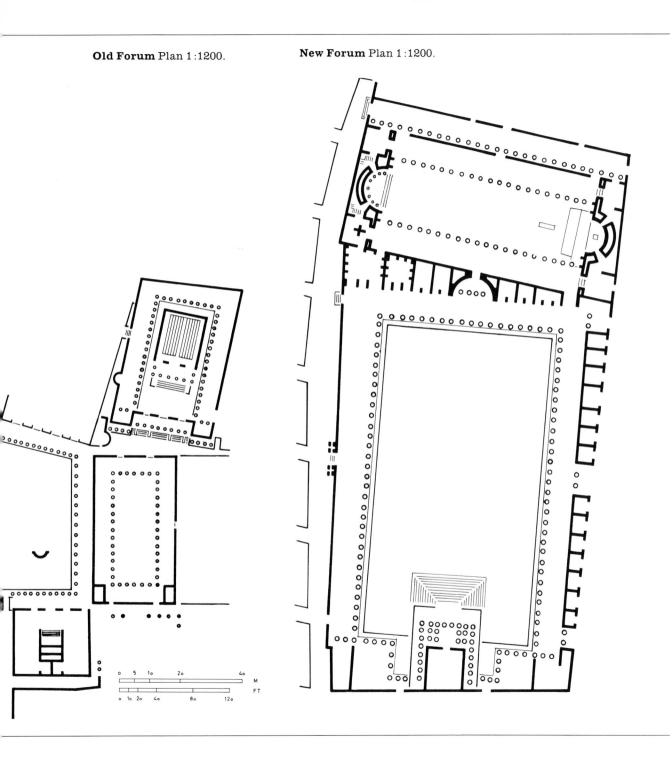

Old Forum Plan 1:1200.   **New Forum** Plan 1:1200.

0 5 1o   2o   4o   M
                                 F T
0 1o 2o 4o   8o   12o

Palmyra

Palmyra, the city of the caravan routes, isolated within its oasis, came within the orbit of the Empire but was never really integrated with it. Its Semitic brand of culture still flourished despite the attraction of Hellenism and, at the same time, the influence of Parthian civilization, which resulted from a synthesis of Iranian and Greek traditions, was as strongly felt as that of the Romans. Thus the architecture of Palmyra can scarcely be said to be Roman, or even of the Roman provincial type. The Temple of Bel, dating from the first half of the first century A.D., combines typically Mesopotamian features such as triangular crenellations with both direct and indirect Hellenistic borrowings. This building, however, shows the rise of a change of taste in the city which was to develop and result, in the second and third centuries, in a compromise style known as Palmyran Classical.

To quote Schlumberger: 'In this phase the outlines and ornament of the old style which were often of Mesopotamian or Iranian origin were replaced in architecture by Greco-Roman forms: tower-tombs were abandoned in favor of tomb-houses or hypogaea, temples were built after Greek models, and streets were ornamented with colonnades like those first found in Antioch. If any reminders survived to recall the architectural taste of the preceding period, they were few and far between and confined to individual details. The commonest of these were probably the heavy consoles which were frequently inserted in the shafts of pilasters or columns to support titular statues.'

This influence of the Mediterranean aesthetic was clearly linked with the political and economic ascendancy of Rome which gained a strong hold in the second century because of the decadence of the Parthian Empire, unable to withstand the attacks of Trajan and Lucius Verus. It is usually considered to have spread from Antioch, but it would be interesting to distinguish between buildings which are purely Roman in style and those which are linked with Hellenistic tradition.

Vitruvius

Marcus Vitruvius Pollio served as an engineer officer in Caesar's armies. After the dictator's death in 44 B.C., he set up as an architect and, about 20 B.C., built a basilica for the town of Fanum which he described in 'De Architectura' (Bk. V, Chapter I). It was at this time he began writing his great treatise.

Despite the reputation he enjoyed in the Renaissance, Vitruvius was not a great architect, and only played a very modest part in the realization of the great building programmes of the Augustan age. Nevertheless, he possessed a sound education, of basically Greek origin, in addition to the practical training he had received as an engineer. He seems to have made a synthesis of several treatises of entirely different periods, thus concocting a kind of eclectic anthology culled from the six preceding centuries. He expressed himself clearly and elegantly and had sufficient scientific knowledge, but he undeniably lacked a wide-ranging intellect and artistic feeling. He has justly been reproached with a lack of understanding of Greek art and, more seriously, for not having realized that an architectural revolution was in progress. As a result he misunderstood the value of fired bricks and almost totally ignored the use of vaults. In his opinion, the Theater of Pompey was a replica of the theater at Mytilene, although, apart from their interior arrangement, there is absolutely no resemblance between them. He did not understand that the substitution of a cavea supported by arches for a hemicycle dug out of a hill radically altered the character of a building. Among the diverse trends constituting Roman architecture, Vitruvius represents the severely classic stream, and no more. The refined, somewhat dry elegance of a monument like the Maison Carrée, whose plan more or less conforms to his precepts, corresponds with his ideal.

The merit of Vitruvius lies in his having been the theorist and legislator of an art whose sphere of application was then being immeasurably enlarged. The perfection of the monuments of Provence dating from the first century would not have been possible without his efforts, which placed the experience accumulated over several centuries by the greatest architects at the disposal of local builders. We must, however, guard against regarding his treatise as a summary of ancient architecture, as has too often been the case between the sixteenth and nineteenth centuries. We must always bear in mind that the greatest and most original creations of Roman architecture occurred after his time and resulted from investigations and researches whose significance he did not understand. This is an insufficiently critical interpretation of the 'De Architectura' which has for too long brought about a completely false idea of a rigidly fixed conception of architecture striving throughout the period of the Empire to reproduce ancient models with ever increasing clumsiness.

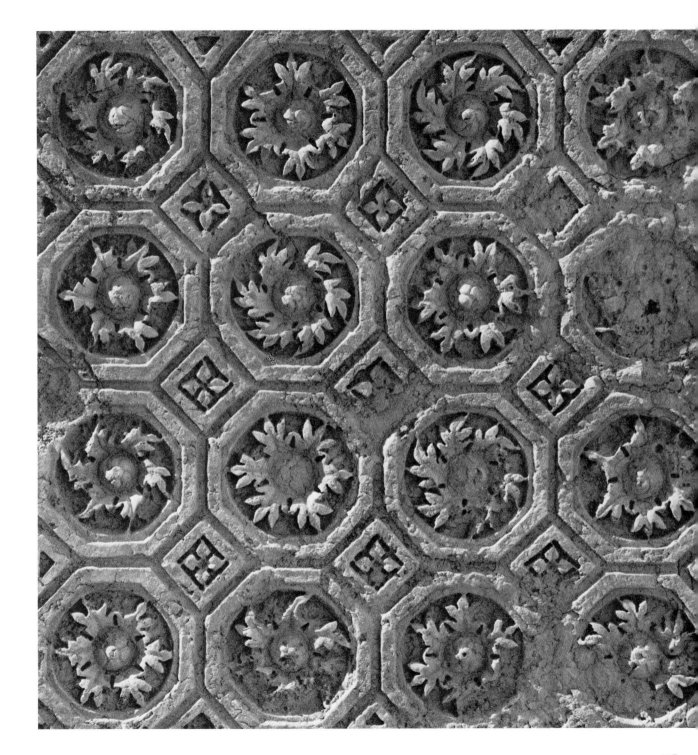

169

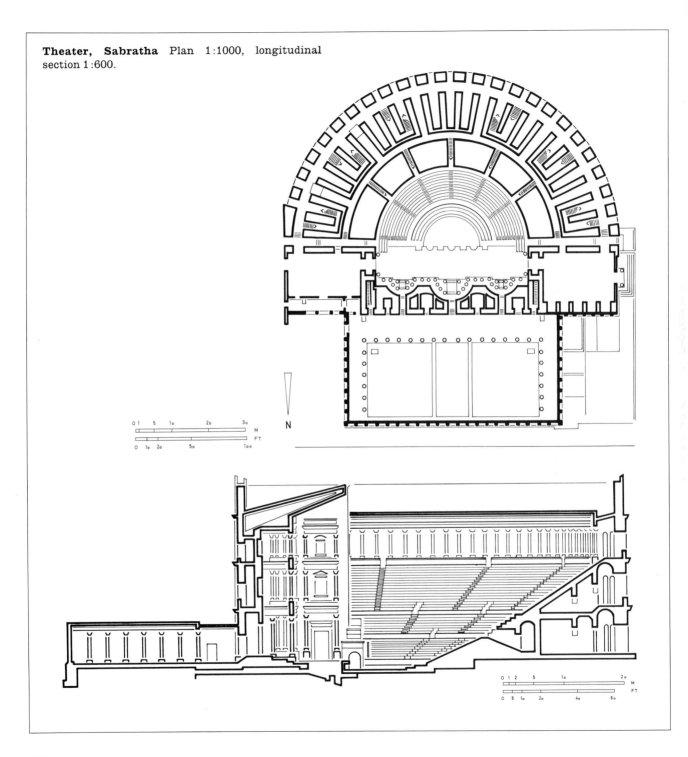

Theater, Sabratha Plan 1:1000, longitudinal
section 1:600.

0 1 5 1o 2o 3o M

0 1o 2o 5o 1oo FT

N

0 1 2 5 1o 2o M

0 5 1o 2o 4o 6o FT

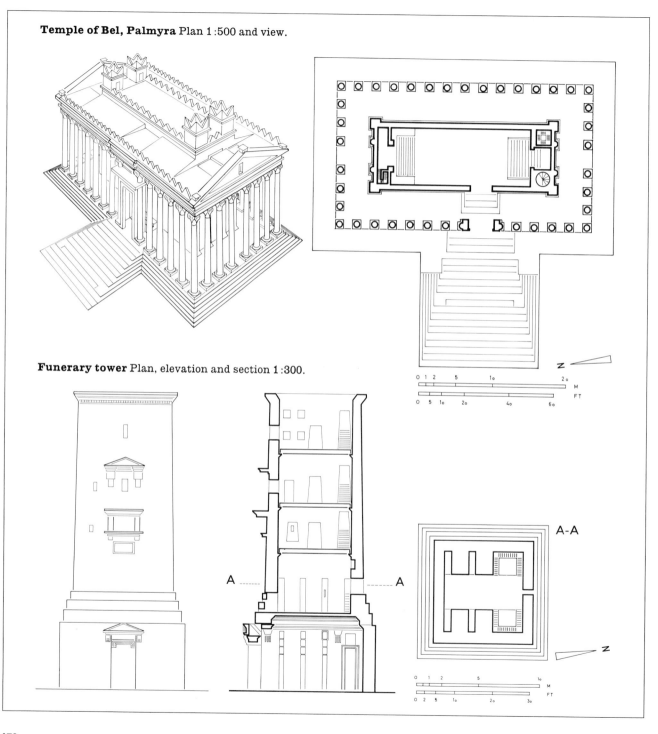

Temple of Bel, Palmyra Plan 1:500 and view.

Funerary tower Plan, elevation and section 1:300.

A-A

5. Symbolism of Roman Architecture

In the course of this book we have had cause to show that a large number of Roman buildings had an ideological significance beyond the practical use to which they were put. We shall now clarify this by examining several monuments whose symbolic value was more important than their practical usefulness.

Triumphal Arches

The illustrations in this book include several examples of triumphal arches: those of Trajan in Timgad, Marcus Aurelius in Tripoli, and of Caracalla in Cuicul (Djemila). These are only a few of a type reappearing throughout the Empire. The most famous examples are those in Rome: the Arches of Titus and Septimius Severus in the Forum Romanum, and the Arch of Constantine near the Colosseum. Another group almost as famous and deservedly so on account of their rich decoration, age and historic interest, are in the South of France at Saint Rémy, Carpentras, Cavaillon and, most notably, Orange.

A triumphal arch is basically a monumental gateway consisting of two massive pylons linked by a semi-circular vault and crowned by an attic, a rectangular mass of masonry designed to carry statues. The arch is framed by two or more columns which are either engaged in the pylons or free-standing on projecting pedestals. They carry an entablature usually quite firmly linked to the structure, passing immediately above the archivolt and separating the attic from the actual opening. There are several possible combinations based on this formula, the first of which are arches with a single bay subdivided into several sections according to the number and disposition of the columns and the details of their ornamentation. There are no arches with two bays. Monuments consisting of twin arches are, in fact, gates, such as the one built by Augustus at Vienne, which is exactly contemporary with the Maison Carrée. The Porta Nigra at Trier is also a development of this formula. (We will presently explain why arches should not be confused with gates.) On the other hand, some of the finest Roman arches, including those of Septimius Severus and Constantine, have three bays. These do not result from the juxtaposition of several arches, but from the piercing of a passage way through the great pylons; the arch at Orange built in the reign of Tiberius is the oldest example of this category. Finally there are the four-sided arches at right-angled cross-roads. These consist of four single-bayed arches joined together. An analysis of the Arch of Marcus Aurelius at Tripoli will show how such compositions were realized.

Until quite recently there have been heated discussions concerning the origins of triumphal arches—some believed that they were of Hellenistic origin while others considered them to be specifically Roman. The problem is now definitely settled in favor of the latter theory and it is possible to retrace their origins exactly.

The excavations carried out in the Forum Romanum just after the end of the Second World War have enabled us to reconstruct the earliest triumphal arch. It was erected between the Temple of Castor and the Temple of Julius Caesar, then occupying the south-east corner of the square, in 29 B.C., and was dedicated to the victor of Actium, then still known as Ceasar Octavian. It was a reproduction on a different scale of an earlier type of monument, again specifically Roman, which made its appearance in the early second century B.C., known as the 'fornix.' The most famous of these was erected by Fabius Maximus in 121 B.C. to commemorate his victories in Gaul. They consisted of an arch and attic, but had no columns: they were also on a comparatively small scale.

Thus a triumphal arch is a special brand of an arch framed by an entablature supported by engaged columns, whose emergence at the end of the second century B.C. was a decisive step in the history of Roman architecture. The significance of the triumphal arch has been as much debated as its origins. The explanation appears to lie in ancient warrior rites going back to the pre-history of the Roman people. At the start of a campaign, magic ceremonies gave warriors a form of destructive rage which would have been just as dangerous for their fellow countrymen as their enemies if they had not been reintegrated into civilian life by means of other rites. One of these consisted in making them pass beneath a sacred gate which released them from this potential destructive force. As they went through they attached to the door-posts, or lintel, the spoils taken from the enemy, or their own weapons which had been rendered taboo by their contact with blood. The memory of these offerings was perpetuated on the monuments of the classical period by the sculptured decoration. Later, the Romans, still keeping the belief that the conquerors were animated by a supernatural force, conceived it not as a passing madness but as a form of grace granted by the gods to certain privileged individuals. The placing of a representation of the victor on the attic clearly proclaimed that he was set above the human race. Triumphal columns surmounted by the statue of an Emperor had the same significance. It is this religious significance which distinguishes arches from mere gateways.

Under the Empire the Emperor became the sole, everlasting conqueror; the generals commanding the armies were no more important than his lieutenants and their success was due to the grace conferred on him by the gods. This power of victory surpassed the human plane and took on cosmic significance. The three African arches which we shall now examine are expressions of this mystic faith.

The Arch of Trajan at Timgad

The arch at Timgad formed the western gateway to Trajan's colony and the inscription carved on the frieze refers to its foundation; hence the reason for its name. Some experts have maintained that it really does date from Trajan's reign, but its direct relation to the 'decumanus maximus' proves that it was included in the overall plan for the city. The main artery was bordered by colonnades in the style of the great avenues of Eastern cities, and the three bays of the arch gave on to the roadway and the pavements sheltered by the arcades. Moreover, the composition of the arch can only be explained with reference to the street. To tie it in more effectively, the architect framed each of the smaller openings with an aedicule which stands out against the mass of the pylon on the side away from the town. The small openings on the other side formed backcloths to the two colonnades. Each of the aedicules consists of two Corinthian columns framing the opening: they are raised on pedestals and support curved pediments. The spaces between the columns above the arches are filled with niches designed to house statues: these are framed by small columns standing on consoles and supporting the underside of a minor entablature. Here again is a type of baroque composition related to the interior decoration of the Temple of Diana at Nîmes and the Temple of Bacchus at Baalbek, both almost contemporary with the arch at Timgad.

The sham colonnades of the Forum Transitorium built at Rome in the reign of Domitian, and the Aula Regia of his palace use similar effects. In each case the columns with their pedestals and related entablatures tend to stand out from the main bulk of the building, forming an independent unit. The Arch of Titus in the Forum Romanum and the Arch of Trajan at Benevento, on the other hand, are representative of a completely different, more usual conception of the triumphal arch. Here the monument forms a homogeneous mass, the architecture of which avoids the spatial division of the plan, in order to accentuate the impression of power. For the same reason, the decoration of these arches consists chiefly of reliefs which enliven their surfaces without destroying their unity, whereas the plastic ornament at Timgad was entirely confined to statues which have, of course, disappeared, apart from a torso which has been replaced in one of the niches. The most notable of these statues must have been the bronze ones on top of the attic. In most other arches this raised pedestal has a vertical rhythm of bays and projections answering the compositional rhythm of the lower section. At Timgad, on the other hand, it consists of a long, rectangular base starting above the pediments of the aedicules, with a molded band with a sharply projecting cornice higher up. This arrangement produces a fresh distribution of light, horizontal instead of vertical, resulting in a contrasting effect between the two sections of the arch.

The attic was probably crowned with a triumphal chariot containing the Emperor and a representation of Victory, with captives or trophies on either side. Coins provide evidence that compositions of this type were erected on the summits of almost every arch, but none has survived: this pattern was inaugurated by Augustus in 19 B.C. when the Arch of Actium which had been built ten years earlier was completely transformed from the commemoration of a civil war to that of a great diplomatic success, the handing over by the Parthians of the standards they had captured from Crassus.

Judging from its proportions, the statue which has been placed in one of the niches of the arch at Timgad must have originally belonged there, and represents Venus. Two octagonal pedestals stand on the east or forward side of the arch. Each of them bears an inscription stating that they were consecrated at the beginning of the third century by an influential citizen, L. Licinius Optatianus, to support statues of Mars and Concord.

This also provides evidence regarding the religious significance of the arch at Timgad, insufficiently explained in the inscription on the frieze. It was really a monument to the cult of

Rome: Tetrapylon of Constantine in the Velabrum (after an engraving by Rossini).

Cuicul (Djemila): elevation and plan of the Arch of Caracalla. About 1:200.

the dynasty, and Venus was represented not so much as the goddess of love but as ancestress of the Roman people and protectress of their Empresses who were compared to her.

Black-and-white photographs give no indication of the color contrasts which contribute to the aesthetic appeal of the arch. Its basic material is limestone which has weathered to a beautiful gold against which the marble of the statue and the small columns stands out, broken by the large dark gaps of the niches and arches. This use of color is also found in Trajan's Markets at Rome and the Horrea Epagathiana at Ostia: it gives meaning to the small columns which would otherwise overload the composition to no purpose.

The Arch of Caracalla at Cuicul (Djemila)

The Arch of Caracalla at Cuicul (Djemila), forming a gateway to the Severan Forum, consists of only one bay framed by projecting features recalling those at Timgad, but treated with a lesser degree of baroque imaginativeness. In this case they comprise two storeys corresponding to the main body of the arch and to the attic. The first is formed of two columns linked by a continuation of the entablature; this gives the aedicule a high degree of unity, but also creates an impression of heaviness which is successfully relieved by the second storey which consists merely of two small columns supporting a miniature pediment without any intervening entablature. The resulting composition is skilfully integrated in the plan of the Severan Forum which, with its irregular shape, gentle slope, well preserved pavement and surrounding buildings blending formality with variety, is perhaps the finest architectural ensemble in Roman Africa.

Tetrapylons or Four-sided Arches

The two arches discussed above consist of two façades with little depth. From the first century onwards, however, attention was paid to the treatment of the lesser sides of these arches. In some cases, inscriptions were carved on them: the Arch of Augustus in the Forum had copies of the victorious Annals of the Republic engraved on its sides. Others were used for decorative purposes: at Carpentras they were carved with bold reliefs explaining the historical significance of the monument, and commemorating the campaigns of Augustus against the Germans and Armenians at the beginning of the Christian era. A more logical solution followed quite naturally when the arch was situated at a

crossroads: it became a tetrapylon, a combination of four gateways. Ancient Oea, which, together with Leptis and Sabratha, made up a confederation of three cities—hence its present name of Tripoli—has kept only one of its monuments intact. This is the four-sided Arch of Marcus Aurelius.

Tripoli: elevation and plan of the Tetrapylon of Marcus Aurelius. About 1:150.

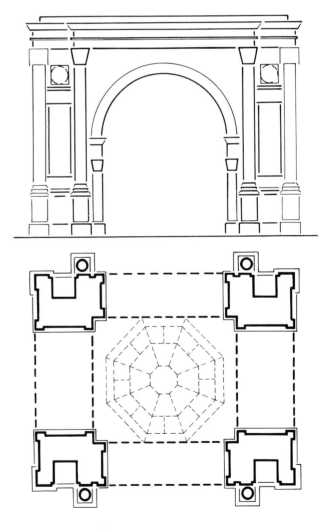

The Latin name for a tetrapylon is synonymous with that of the oldest and most mysterious god in the Roman pantheon: Janus. The original nature of this deity has been much debated, but it is known that he presided over the early history of the nation and that his shrine in the Forum essentially consisted of a door which was opened in time of war and closed when peace was concluded.

The Tetrapylon of Marcus Aurelius at Tripoli

The Temple of Janus in the Forum has completely disappeared, so its exact shape is not known. There are, however, several examples of four-sided arches in a good state of preservation, including one at Cavaillon dating from the end of the reign of Augustus. The Janus at Tripoli stands in the center of the city near a temple dedicated to the tutelary deity of the colony, which was built about twenty years later. It is composed entirely of Greek marble, a most unusual extravagance, and is sited at the crossing of two streets. The plan consists of four rectangular pylons each of which has a deep, shadowy niche hollowed out on its main front; the arches on the main fronts were flanked by two free-standing columns carrying the underside of an entablature. Inside, an octagonal drum rests on pillars and arches and supports a shallow dome with carved coffers on the inner surface. The form taken by the exterior superstructure is by no means certain. Some think there may have been a lofty octagonal pavilion crowned by a dome similar to the tower of the Conocchia at Capua, others that it consisted of a flattened dome. In any case it is probable that there was a statue on the summit. What is certain is that the arch had no attic, a feature which distinguished it from the Severan tetrapylons at Leptis and Tebessa. The former had an attic with sculptured friezes representing historical subjects, while that of the latter was surmounted by aedicules similar to those on the arch at Cuicul, so that their inner domes were concealed.

The sculptured decoration of the arch at Tripoli is very rich and highly interesting. The spandrels on the main fronts are ornamented with winged Victories and the niches, which used to house statues of the Emperors, are crowned by badly mutilated busts. These, by their number, arrangement, and association with the Victories, may be identified as the Seasons. Victories and Seasons may also be found in close proximity on the Arches of Trajan at Benevento, and of Septimius Severus and Constantine at Rome. The lesser façades where the absence of columns and niches allowed a clearer field were covered with huge bas-reliefs, but these now only remain on the north side. Further down the pylon are trophies with two captive barbarians at their feet, and on the spandrels above, two chariots speed upwards: the one on the right carries Minerva, the one on the left, Apollo, the classical equivalents of the ancient Phoenician divinities who protected Oea. Here they are represented setting out to war in support of the Roman armies, and their enthusiasm symbolizes the loyalty of the native population.

The non-figurative decoration is of extreme elegance: notable features are the vine scrolls deeply incised in the carved angle pillars, the bunches of acanthus surrounding the bases of the shafts (as in the Nymphaeum at Nîmes), and the heart-shaped ornaments above their pedestals. This wealth of decoration is typical of African art dating from the period of the late Antonine and Severan Emperors.

C. Calpurnius Celsus, magistrate of Oea, presented this magnificent arch to Marcus Aurelius and his adopted brother, Lucius Verus, in 163 A.D. The tetrapylon at Tripoli is one of the

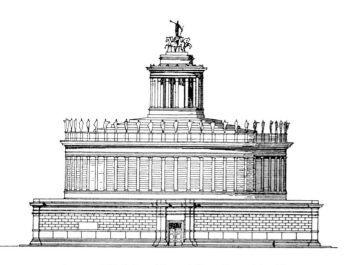

Mausoleum of Hadrian (Castel Sant'Angelo). About 1:1000.

most remarkable monuments of the political ideology of the Empire. It bears witness to the union of the earliest religious traditions of the Mediterranean with the humanist ideals of an aristocracy schooled in a pantheistic syncretism.

Tombs and Monuments Commemorating Victories

This relationship between a state religion which had lost the inhuman coldness of its Augustan prototype, and spiritual doctrines

Mausoleum at S. Maria Capua Vetere, known as the 'Carceri Vecchie' (after Pane).

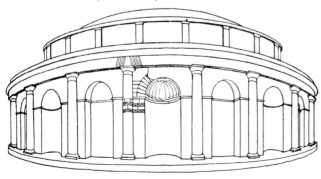

holding forth promises of a happy everlasting life explains the striking similarity between monuments commemorating victories, and tombs. This is an aspect of Roman cities which we have not so far discussed but which must now be examined. Every town was surrounded by a necropolis on a grand scale: these were not cut off from the world like our enclosed cemeteries, but lay along the sides of the roads where the monuments attracted attention by their epitaphs.

Only one of these Roman mausolea will be examined here, the Conocchia at Capua, noteworthy both because of its strange situation and its perfect state of preservation. It was probably built towards the end of the first century A.D. and stands on the edge of the Appian Way near S. Maria Capua Vetere, the site of the capital of Campania: the city was destroyed by the Romans as a punishment for having opened its gates to Hannibal, but its ruins were later restored. The monument consists of three storeys including a square base, a curvilinear pedestal and a round tower. The pedestal contains the funerary chambers, the rest is solid masonry with a purely ornamental function.

On account of its overall plan, the Conocchia may be included in a type of mausoleum that could be found throughout the entire Mediterranean world. Its origin may probably be traced to Western Asia Minor: it was, in fact, usual for the rulers of these regions to build themselves monumental tombs in the form of pillars which, from the fifth century onwards, were decorated by Greek artists. The fame of the Mausoleum of Halicarnassus erected by Artemisia, Queen of Caria, in memory of her husband in 353 A.D. and considered one of the seven wonders of the world, caused the spread of this type of monument right across the Hellenistic world as far as the western Mediterranean basin. The two commonest forms of Roman mausolea are either

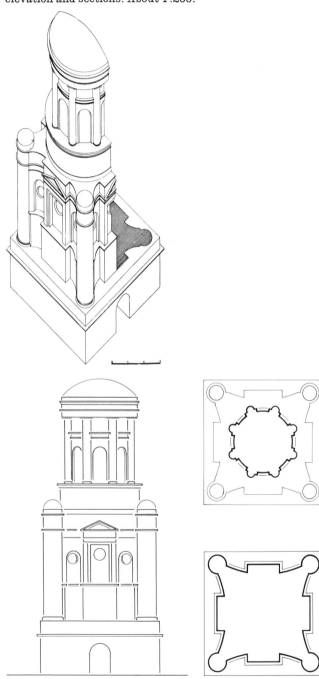

massive rotundas such as the Mausolea of Augustus, and of Hadrian (now the Castel Sant' Angelo), or slim towers. These two types also occur simultaneously in a variety of Mediterranean civilizations. Heavy rotundas, which were really mounds of earth translated into monumental form, were already known to the Etruscans, and the strange tombs of the Numidian kings also belong to the same category. Another example is the Carceri Vecchie near Capua where the drum is formed of alternate courses of stone and brick and receives its exterior rhythm from arches framed by pilasters: it contains a funerary chamber of cruciform plan, reached by a long corridor.

Gateway to the Other World

It is under this heading that the Conocchia belongs; and its division into three storeys is found again at Saint-Rémy and in many other tombs. In this we can see the distant influence of the Mausoleum of Halicarnassus, a funerary temple crowned with a pyramidal roof and set on a raised pedestal. Each storey has a symbolic significance, clearly apparent at Saint-Rémy in the sculptured decorations, and surviving to a lesser degree in the Conocchia. The pedestal of the latter enclosed the funerary chamber designed to shelter the mortal remains of the dead—in other words, the urns containing their ashes—and, at Saint-Rémy, their life on earth was symbolically represented by the sculptures on the walls. The second storey represents the glorification of the dead and their passing to the next life: hence the importance of the theme of the gateway whose basic significance in Roman art has already been stressed. The architect at Saint-Rémy very cleverly gave this section of his monument the form of a four-sided arch, thus suggesting the idea of triumph and at the same time lightening his composition.

At Capua the architect devised another

solution. Each side of the monument has an inward curve bounded at the corners by small round towers. In the center projects a pedimented aedicule flanked by arcaded niches. The resulting sense of movement gives the building its chief attraction, and recalls that of city gates set in a semi-circle with towers on either side. This derivation has been confirmed from representations on funerary urns such as that of Volusia Arbuscula which shows a Silenus entering the gate of the underworld framed by small twisted columns which produce the same baroque sense of movement as the Conocchia. The aedicules at Capua thus represent gateways to the other world depicted as a fortress, an idea as common in antiquity as in the Middle Ages.

There was probably a secondary reason which contributed to the architect's choice of an inward curve for the faces of his second storey. Several mausolea include, at ground level, a semi-circular exedra which is really a seat designed so that passers by may rest and meditate near the dead. Such seats often formed part of the funerary gardens surrounding monumental mausolea.

The third storey, taken on its own, forms a small round temple. It is both the sanctuary of the deified dead and a symbolic representation of the heaven where they live for eternity. The development of this section of the monuments is as strange and complex as that of the others. The Mausoleum of Halicarnassus consisted of a square funerary temple crowned by a pyramidal roof and set on a lofty pedestal forming the bottom storey of the composition. The Greeks, however, preferred their sanctuaries of the dead to have the circular plan of the 'tholoi' originally dedicated to the gods of the earth, whose cult bore a marked resemblance to that of the dead. In later versions of the mausoleum, a 'tholos' very often took the place of a square temple, which had the additional advantage of increasing the variety of the composition. Under the Empire there was a very frequent tendency to forget the difference between the cults of heroes and of gods. The 'tholos,' however, took on a fresh significance, recalling the vault of heaven by its circular shape. In the Hellenistic period, the home of the happy dead was no longer placed in the underworld: under the influence of eschatology and Eastern religions, they were believed to have been transported into the upper reaches of the firmament near the stars. Henceforward, the 'tholos' symbolized this final phase of human destiny—the well-earned paradise of virtuous souls.

The Significance of Trajan's Column

Trajan's Column is another example of the relationship between tombs and monuments

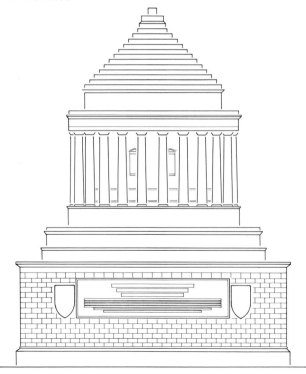

Elevation of the Tropaeum at La Turbie near Nice. About 1:450.

commemorating victories. It is, in fact, a combination of both, and is similar in signific-ance to the Conocchia at Capua. The base of the column housed the ashes of the Emperor and the tall shaft with its long sculptured spiral—a real tapestry in stone—represents both the historical event of Trajan's conquest of Dacia and his individual struggle to be worthy of his own deification. It is highly significant to note that the main themes of the long frieze, chosen as much for their illustrations of model virtues as for their historic interest, may be found again in the decoration of sarcophagi of members of the aristocracy.

The Tropaea

There are other strictly architectural features which subscribe to the same dicta. These include the monumental 'tropaea' whose main purpose was to commemorate a victory or conquest of arms. They are so like mausolea that it is practically impossible to distinguish one from the other in cases where inscriptions and decoration have vanished. Two Roman 'tropaea' are particularly well preserved. One of these is at La Turbie near Nice: it dates from the time of Augustus and commemorates the pacification of the Alps. Jules Formigé, who was responsible for its restoration, has found that the guiding principles of the Mausoleum of Halicarnassus are embodied in its plan. The other was built by Trajan at Adamklissi in the Dobrudja to glorify the conquest of Dacia, and belongs to the type of massive rotundas.

The most remarkable feature of the Conocchia at Capua is that the architect, in his desire to express the ideology of his time, was led to the choice of baroque forms. In this case, too, the use of the term is justified both from the aesthetic standpoint and from an exact histor-ical parallel, inasmuch as Borromini later adopted the same solutions for the campanile and cupola of Sant' Andrea delle Frate. The façade of Sant' Agnese in the Piazza Navona, Borromini's most famous work, was also built to exactly the same design as the middle storey of the Conocchia.

CONCLUSION

In our analysis of some of the most character-istic monuments of Roman architecture, we have noted the development of three tendencies: functionalism, classicism, and baroque. The second of these appears to be strictly linked with one personality—that of Augustus. It is, for instance, more or less impossible to talk of the classicist tendencies of Hadrian, as C. C. van Essen, one of the greatest experts on Roman art, pointed out.

Hadrian's reign, he wrote, was the last occasion on which Greek art exercised a direct influence on that of the Romans. An overall analysis of the artistic climate reveals, however, that it already showed a difference from that of the Augustan age. However, I feel that Roman classicism was not a reproduction of Hellenism. It is true that Greek art never ceased to exert its influence on that of Rome, but this was never strong enough to strangle the original trends expressing the thought of the period. We must bear in mind that classicism, despite its tempor-ary brilliance, was no more than a passing phenomenon in Rome's artistic development.

If we follow the example of the humanist scholars and base our survey of the history of Latin civilization wholly on literary texts (al-though from a critical point of view), we shall come to see the century of Augustus neither as the apogée of this civilization, nor as the start of a long period of decadence, but rather as the beginning of an era of maturity which reached its peak in the second century and, having survived a crisis, carried on till the end of the fourth century. Classicism thus regains its rightful place as just one episode in the formation of the Roman genius, comparable with the part played by the literary and artistic development of sixteenth century France.

It remains to consider the other two tendencies, functionalism and Baroque, both permanent and fundamental. We have already seen that, far from being in opposition, they complement one another so perfectly that almost all the notable creations of Roman architecture share a functional and a baroque aspect. The former represents the practical side of the Romans. It is displayed in their first attempts at architecture and continues until the end of the Empire. The baroque aspect on the other hand, expresses their feeling for magnificence, unknown to their early ancestors, and which did not develop until their conquest of the Hellenistic world.

There really must have been constructions designed to curvilinear plans in the Hellenistic world, and we may perhaps gain an idea of what they were like from the architectural landscapes of the second Pompeian style, even though the style itself appears typically Italian. They must all, however, have been limited to imaginative constructions such as garden pavilions, pleasure-boats, and temporary festival decorations executed in light, non-durable materials. It was the technique of the Romans that enabled these bold formulae, defying gravity and toughness of materials, to be solidly expressed; technique allowed them to use rubble construction and resolve the problems of dynamics in such a way as to reduce a building to its points of support. These formulae were henceforward used in all buildings designed as public amenities—the most original aspect of Imperial social policy.

This way of life, though based on a wholly agrarian economy, was strangely similar to certain aspects of our industrial civilization, and was clearly only capable of realization because of the Pax Romana. When this was dangerously disturbed, the mode of life it supported was naturally condemned. Thus, from the beginning of the fourth century, we find a radical change in building programmes. From now on money was devoted to military works, buildings connected with the Christian faith, and imperial and noble palaces. Although efforts were, in fact, made to preserve some public buildings—such as baths and circuses—in the devastated regions it was very often impossible to rebuild them, and there was no hesitation about re-using portions of them in the ramparts—which fortunately preserved them.

It is also interesting to note that, apart from a few examples in the most important cities, the baths built in the fourth, and still more in the fifth and sixth centuries, were designed with a thriftiness which makes them seem rather mean when compared with the vast thermae of the second and third centuries. This change resulted more from a desire to save on water and fuel than from a decline in architectural technique. As regards town-planning, every effort was directed to make the utmost use of the ground. In such cases it was necessary to do away with most of the open spaces—square, avenues, courtyards, and gardens—which had made the cities of the High Empire look so attractive.

It is not surprising to find that these changes were accompanied by a simplification of technique, especially in the West. An interesting fact is that, after the building of the Basilica of Maxentius, scarcely any other large vaulted halls were constructed, and the Christian churches in the Latin provinces were given timber roofs from the time of Constantine onwards. Baroque effects were still to be found, however. They blended only too well with court ceremonial, which reached fresh heights of elegance at this time, and with the Christian liturgy, which borrowed the major part of its ritual from court pageantry.

Yet the technical discoveries of the Roman period were not utterly lost. Byzantine architects pursued their researches in fresh directions, devoting themselves especially to the problems of domes, but the Romans, despite their reliance on single stones and rubble fillings, had already outlined the two solutions which were to be required for this type of vault. Pendentives are to be found in some second century mausolea and in the Baths of Caracalla, and squinches were used in the construction of the tetrapylon at Tebessa. Even in the West, dominated by the Germans from the fifth century, their basic techniques were not forgotten.

In this way the legacy of Roman architecture was quite naturally passed on to the different civilizations of the Middle Ages, both Christian and Moslem. In addition, there were also the technical discoveries made by the archaeologists of the Renaissance and the seventeenth and eighteenth centuries. The importance of these has already been stressed. We must, however, finally correct a common error: it is that of seeing the basic tenets of Roman Imperial architecture reflected in the neo-classic buildings of the nineteenth century. The Pantheon and the Madeleine in Paris, the Victor Emmanuel Monument in Rome, whether or not they are successful as buildings, have captured none of the mysterious and wonderful atmosphere created by the great Roman architects with their baths, basilicas and palaces.

This atmosphere could not possibly have been recreated in a civilization far removed from the strange, complex ideology which inspired it originally—an ideology which we can only understand with difficulty and of whose existence the rationalist philosophers of the eighteenth century were completely ignorant.

Chronological Table ▶

Chronological Table

Dates	Events	Monuments
B.C.		
753 (April 21)	Varronian date for the foundation of Rome.	Huts on the Palatine. Necropolis on the site of the Forum.
c. 600 (?)	The Etruscans in Rome.	Cloaca Maxima.
c. 550	Servius Tullius.	Enclosure of the city. Temples in the Forum and Forum Boarium.
509	Fall of the Tarquins.	Capitol.
c. 390	Invasion of the Gauls.	Rebuilding of the city wall.
343	Alliance of Rome with Campania.	Castrum of Ostia.
Until 291	Samnite wars.	Foundation of Alba Fucens (303).
280	War with Pyrrhus.	Tomb of the Scipios.
264-202	First and second Punic wars.	First temples on the Largo Argentina.
2nd century	Conquest of the Mediterranean basin.	Ionic temple on the Forum Boarium. Temple of Veiovis on the Capitol. Samnite homes at Herculaneum and Pompeii. Roman houses on Delos.
83-79	Dictatorship of Sulla.	Tabularium. Sanctuary at Praeneste. Basilica and House of the Faun at Pompeii. Sulla's house at Glanum.
62	Triumph of Pompey.	Theater of Pompey.
49-44	Dictatorship of Caesar	Forum of Caesar. Temple of Venus Genetrix.
43-31	Second triumvirate.	Temple of Valetudo at Glanum (39). Temple of Julius Caesar.
31 (Sept. 2)	Battle of Actium.	Arch of Augustus in the Forum (29, restored in 19). Temple of Apollo Palatinus (28). Arch of Augustus at Rimini (27). Mausoleum of the Julii at Glanum. Pont du Gard. Cryptoportici at Arles.
27 (January 13)	Octavius receives the name of Augustus.	Nymphaeum at Nîmes. Theater of Marcellus. Temple of Apollo in the Prata Flaminia. Maison Carrée at Nîmes.
13	Return of Augustus to Rome from Gaul.	Ara Pacis. Forum of Augustus. Temple of Mars Ultor.

Dates	Events	Monuments
A.D. 14-37	Reign of Tiberius.	Completion of the Theater at Leptis Magna. Arch at Orange. Grotto at Sperlonga. Temple of Bel at Palmyra. Great temple at Baalbek.
41-54	Reign of Claudius.	During these reigns, the third style of Pompeian paintings.
54-68	Reign of Nero.	Domus Aurea (after 63). Fourth Pompeian style.
69-96	Flavian Dynasty: Vespasian, Titus and Domitian.	Destruction of Pompeii and Herculaneum (79). Temple of Diana at Nîmes. Inauguration of the Colosseum (80). Domus Flavia on the Palatine (completed in 92).
98-117	Reign of Trajan.	Forum and Markets of Trajan (from 106). Foundation of Timgad (100).
117-138	Hadrian.	Hadrian's Villa at Tibur. Pantheon. Temple of Venus and Rome. Large-scale development at Ostia: Horrea Epagathiana.
138-161 161-180 180-192	Antoninus Pius. Marcus Aurelius. Commodus.	In the course of these reigns, large-scale development in architecture and town-planning throughout the provinces. In particular, building of the Temple of Bacchus at Baalbek. Spread of the type of the Imperial thermae.
192-235	Severan Dynasty.	Forum, basilica, and arch at Leptis Magna. Theater at Sabratha. Baths of Caracalla. Amphitheater at El-Djem. Oil factory at Brisgane.
235-284	Military anarchy.	Fortified wall round Rome.
284-305	Tetrarchy.	Palaces at Spalato (Split) and Piazza Armerina. Monuments of Galerus at Salonika. Baths of Diocletian. Basilica of Maxentius (306-311).

Bibliography

General Works on Roman Civilization

Aymard, André et Auboyer, Jeannine
Rome et son Empire. Paris, Presses Universitaires, 1954

Grenier, Albert
Le Génie Romain dans la Religion, la Pensée et l'Art.
Paris, Presses Universitaires, 1954.

Grimal, Pierre
La Civilisation Romaine. Paris, Arthaud, 1960

Picard, Gilbert Charles
La Civilisation de L'Afrique Romaine. Paris, Plon, 1959.

General Works on Roman Art with Emphasis on Architecture

Becatti, Giovanni
L'Arte Romana. Milano, Garzanti, 1962

Essen, Charles Claude van
Précis d'Histoire de l'Art Antique en Italie. Bruxelles,
Latomus, 1960

Garcia y Bellido, Antonio
L'Arte Romano. Madrid, Enciclopedia Clasica, 1963

Kähler, Heinz
Rom und sein Imperium. Baden-Baden, Holle Verlag, 1962

Picard, Gilbert Charles
L'Art Romain. Paris, Presses Universitaires, 1962

Picard, Gilbert Charles
L'Art Etrusque et Romain. Paris, Charles Massin, 1964

Schefold, Karl
Romische Kunst als Religioses Phänomen. Hamburg,
Rowohlt, 1963

Treatises on Roman Architecture

Choisy, Auguste
L'Art de bâtir chez les Romains. Paris 1873

Crema, Luigi
L'Architettura Romana. Torino, Societa Edetrice Internazionale, 1959 (basic work)

Lugli, Giuseppe
La Tecnica edilizi romana, con particolare riguardo a
Roma e Lazio. Roma, Bardi, 1957

Robertson, Donald Struan
A Handbook of Greek and Roman Architecture. Cambridge
University Press, 1945

General Works on Roman Monuments

Lugli, Giuseppe
I monumente antiche di Roma e Sub urbio. Roma, Bardi,
1932-1938

Lugli, Giuseppe
Roma Antica, Il centro monumentale. Roma, Bardi, 1946

Platner, Samuel Ball and Ashby, Thomas
A Topographical Dictionary of Ancient Rome. Oxford and
London University Press, 1929

Chapter 1: Structure and Function of the City

Bianchi Bandinelli, Ranuccio; Caffarelli, Ernesto Vergara;
Caputo, Giacomo
Leptis Magna. Verona, 1964

Boethius, Axel
The Neronian Nova Urbs, Corolla Gustav Adolpho. Lund,
1932 p. 84 sqq (and numerous other articles)

Courtois, Christian
Timgad antique Thamugadi. Algiers, 1951

Grimal, Pierre
Les Villes Romaines. Paris, Presses Universitaires, 1954

Gsell, Stephane
Afrique, Monuments antiques de L'Algérie. Paris 1901

Homo, Leon
Rome imperiale et l'Urbanisme dans l'Antiquité. Paris, Albin Michel 1951

Lavedan, Pierre
Histoire de l'Urbanisme dans l'Antiquité. Paris, Henri Laurens, 1926

Chapter II: Functional Architecture cf. Bibliography for **Chapter III: From Classicism to Baroque**

Balty, Jean Charles
Etudes sur la Maison Carrée de Nîmes. Bruxelles, Latomus, 1960

Charbonneaux, Jean
L'Art Romain au siecle d'Auguste. Lausanne, Guilde du Livre, 1948

Kähler, Heinz
Die römischen Kapitelle des Rheingebietes. Berlin, 1939

Kraus, Theodor
Die Ranken der Ara Pacis. Berlin, Mann, 1953

Krencker, Daniel et Zschietzschmann, Willy
Römische Tempel in Syrien. Berlin, de Gruyter, 1938

Naumann, Rudolf
Der Quellbezirk von Nîmes. (Denkmäler antiker Architektur). Berlin, 1932

Wiegand, Theodor
Baalbek. Berlin and Leipzig, de Gruyter, 1921

Chapter IV: Private and Public Amenities

Boethius, Axel
The Golden House of Nero. Ann Arbor, 1960

Kähler, Heinz
Hadrian und seine Villa bei Tivoli. Berlin, 1959

Krencker, Daniel et Kruger, Emil
Die Trierer Kaiserthermen. Augsburg, 1929

Meiggs, Russell
Roman Ostia. Oxford, Clarendon Press, 1960

Spinazzola, Vittorio
Pompei alla luce degli Scavi nuovi di Via dell'Abbondanza. Roma, Libreria dello Stato, 1957 (of equal importance for streets and façades)

Tamm, Birgitta
Auditorium and Palatium. Stockholm, 1963

Chapter V: Symbolism of Roman Architecture

Amy, Robert; Duval, Paul-Marie; Formigé, Jules; Hatt, Jean Jacques; Picard, Gilbert Charles; Pignaniol, André
L'Arc d'Orange. Paris, CNRS, 1962

Franciscis, Alfonso de, et de Pane, Roberto
Mausolei Romani in Campania. Naples, Ed. Scient. Ital. 1957

Kähler, Heinz
article "Triumphbogen" in Realencyclopaedie der classischen Altertumswissenschaft, Vol VII A I

Mansuelli, Guido Achille
Il Monumento Augusteo del 27 a C. Nuovo ricerche sull' Arco di Rimini. Bologna 1960

L'Orange, Hans Peter et Gerkan, Armin von
Der spätantike Bildschmuck des Konstantinsbogens. Berlin, 1939

Picard, Gilbert Charles
Les Trophées Romaines. Paris, de Boccard, 1957

Hatt, Jean Jacques
La Tombe gallo-romaine. Paris, Presses Universitaires, 1951

Cumont, Franz
Recherches sur le symbolisme funéraire des Romains. Paris, Geutner, 1947 (This deals mainly with interpretations of sculptures and also with all aspects of symbolism.)

N.B. This bibliography only refers to general works containing references to more detailed studies and earlier writings.

Table of Contents

Plans accompanying text

Plates

Jacket: detail of arch and horizontal course bordering courtyard of the Oil Factory at Brisgane

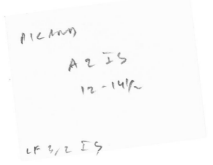